Shared **Responsibility**

Shared

Responsibility

Beating bullying in
Australian schools

IAN FINDLEY

ACER Press

First published 2006
by ACER Press
Australian Council *for* Educational Research Ltd
19 Prospect Hill Road, Camberwell, Victoria 3124

Edited by Susannah Burgess
Cover and text design by R.T.J. Klinkhamer
Cover illustration by Steven Hallam
Typeset by J&M Typesetting
Printed by Hyde Park Press

National Library of Australia Cataloguing-in-Publication data:
  Findley, Ian.
    Shared responsibility : beating bullying in Australian
    schools.

  ISBN 0 86431 477 9.

  1. Bullying in schools - Australia. 2. Bullying in schools
  - Australia - Prevention. 3. Children - Counseling of. 4.
  Problem children - Behavior modification. I. Title.

  371.580994

Visit our website: www.acerpress.com.au

CONTENTS

ABOUT THE AUTHOR

Ian is a family man with four grown-up children. He graduated from La Trobe University with a BA in Religious Studies and Music. Ian has worked in secondary schools for twenty-seven years as a teacher, a coordinator, and for the past twelve years as a CCES accredited Chaplain in state secondary schools.

Ian loves music, people and particularly working with teenagers. As a chaplain he has spent many hours pastorally caring for staff, students and their families. He is a keen observer of human behaviour and has identified ways of connecting and communicating with people of all ages. Ian's insight and understanding of the issues relating to bullying has enabled him to see beyond the surface and to connect with those young people who have been the recipients of bullying as well as with those who engage in it.

Ian is a gifted storyteller, writer and teacher who uses story to capture and grip the reader while skilfully intertwining it with teaching the method.

ACKNOWLEDGEMENTS

I would like to acknowledge some very special people who have encouraged and supported me in my research and writing of this book.

My Principal Avril Salter has allowed me the freedom to experiment within her school and develop a method that has proven very effective in beating bullying. Avril also took an active role in proofreading the material and getting the word out there so other schools can benefit from this method.

I thank my many colleagues at Whittlesea Secondary College for feedback and valuable support. I particularly acknowledge and thank Anna Secondi for the many hours she put in proofreading the text and providing valuable insight and feedback into how I should write. I also thank Robert Cole for the time he gave that helped me express my ideas in an appropriate and acceptable way.

I thank Lt Colonel Pam Trigg who not only assisted in the pre-editing process but also became fired up about the book's possibilities and encouraged me to get it published.

I thank my editor Susannah Burgess for all her hard work in preparing this book for publication.

I thank my wife Julie for her support and patience during the time it took to write and prepare this book. She was invaluable for bouncing ideas off and proofreading the material.

In all the support I have had, there is one person who lies behind this book from its inception. This is my good friend and colleague Jenice Stokes without whom this book would have never been written. It was Jenice who noticed the power and effectiveness of the method in beating bullying and insisted that I write it down so other schools may benefit. It was Jenice who managed and set out the processes of the book's structure. It was Jenice who promoted and pushed forward to ensure that this book became a reality. It was Jenice who encouraged me to keep going when I was feeling that writing was not my thing. I dedicate this book to her and all the students who have found themselves on the receiving end of hurtful, cruel bullying. It is my prayer that what I have learnt and shared in this book will assist many to heal, and then rise above and beat bullying.

INTRODUCTION

I am writing this book because I need your help to solve a problem, a big problem, the problem of 'bullying in schools'. It is my hope that after reading this book you will assist me by sharing the responsibility in combating this serious problem, a problem that has plagued schools since community schooling began.

I cannot do it alone, I need your help. If we work together I'm sure we will discover ways that will ensure the safety of the victims and put a stop to bullying.

As a teenager I was both a bully and a victim, so I know what it is like on both sides of the fence. In twenty-seven years of teaching and working in secondary schools, I have encountered and responded to many incidents of bullying, but it wasn't until I became a School Chaplain in 1993 that the seriousness of bullying really hit home to me. As a chaplain I got to hear many of the usually untold stories that lie behind the sad, sometimes helpless eyes of the victims. I became privy to the pain of those who had been subjected to cruel, hurtful, sometimes spirit-breaking acts of bullying.

Over the years schools have struggled to know how to ensure both the safety and a feeling of safety for the students who have been the unfortunate recipients of bullying. Schools have been largely ineffective in changing the behaviour of those who bully others. In addition to this, schools have failed to provide effective support programs that assist the wounded students to recover, heal, and rise above bullying.

Schools have traditionally tried to overcome bullying with a 'fix the bully' type mentality. Since the rise in awareness of the impact of bullying in our schools, governments have required all schools to have a 'bullying policy' in place. Schools now boast of policies that do not tolerate bullying. Some are even bold enough to make claims of having a 'bully free' school. No schools are 'bully free'. Bullying is a social phenomenon. It occurs when people are grouped together and battle for recognition, power and social position. The policy is not what is important. What is important is the procedure: the method the school uses to respond to and deal with bullying incidents. It is the procedure that gives life, power and meaning to the policy. It is the procedure that either succeeds or fails.

Schools aim to provide a learning environment where students are safe and feel safe, and where bullying incidents are dealt with efficiently and effectively.

Shared responsibility is a practical procedure that makes it possible to achieve this aim.

The aim is threefold and ensures:

- students are safe,
- students feel safe,
- bullying is stopped.

This book is the product of twelve years research, twenty-seven years experience in secondary schools and much heart wrenching experimentation. The motivation for writing this book is compassion for the weak and the hurting as well as a desire to share what I have found to be effective with others. It has been written in, and for, Australian schools. I acknowledge the influence of the writing and work of Barbara Maines and George Robinson who developed the 'No Blame Approach' to overcoming bullying in England.[1]

In writing this book, I have integrated theory and practice into story. As a teacher and a preacher, I am a storyteller. I have experienced considerable success communicating using this genre and it is my hope that I can connect with you through the stories in this book. The stories in this book are real stories about real people, but the names and some of the details have been changed for privacy reasons.

What is shared responsibility?

Shared responsibility is putting a stop to bullying. It has as the core component the Shared Responsibility Meeting. This is a powerful and effective interviewing process that puts an immediate stop to bullying. The process appeals to empathy by putting a *real person* with *real feelings* in the place of the *object victim*.

Shared responsibility is looking after the needs of victims. It facilitates healing, assists recovery and develops the needed confidence and skills that enable students to cope and survive in a competitive school environment. It teaches students how to be, and feel, safe.

Shared responsibility is a proven, positive, powerful, effective approach to beating bullying in schools.

Shared responsibility is a proactive, whole school approach to beating bullying in Australian schools.

Shared responsibility is inviting the whole school community to share the responsibility for creating and maintaining an educational environment that is happy and safe for all students.

---

[1] Babara Maines and George Robinson developed and published the 'No Blame Approach' in dealing with bullying in England. It was published in the UK by Lucky Duck Press Ltd
www.luckyduck.com.uk It was later published with permission in Australia by Inyahead Press
www.inyahead.com.au

Shared responsibility is built on concepts of welfare, education and discipline.

- Welfare:
  - takes into account the needs of all students
  - supports all students
  - treats all students with equal respect

- Education:
  - teaches responsibility, values and life skills
  - teaches an understanding of bullying
  - teaches the potential impact of bullying
  - teaches school policy and procedures

- Discipline:
  - fosters self-discipline and self-control
  - incorporates consequence for actions

Shared responsibility is simple, straightforward, and can be managed by anyone who has basic people skills.

Shared responsibility empowers students to act.

Ian Findley
Melbourne

PART ONE

Shared Responsibility

CHAPTER ONE
THE IMPACT OF BULLYING

Bullying has more victims than just the initial target.

It is 9:20 on Monday morning, 26 February 1993. I am sitting in my office at my new school planning the activities of the day when there is a knock at my door. I look up, the door opens, and in walks a woman who I have never met before. She greets me with a question. 'Are you the new Chaplain?' She looks nervous, upset and a little panicky. Her eyes are sad and I can see she is fighting hard to hold back the tears that are welling up within them. Closing the door, I invite her to sit down. She cannot contain her tears any longer and begins to sob uncontrollably. From amid the tears and sobs I hear, 'Why? Why did he do it? Why did he do this to me?'

Slowly she began to tell her story.

> It was two years ago now, on a Friday night. We all had our different things to do on Fridays so we generally looked after ourselves and got our own tea. Friday was my night off. Bill had been down at the radio station, Jeremy was out with his mates and Liam had been for his usual run, come home, made a sandwich, left his usual mess on the bench and gone to his room. It was just after eleven when I decided to go to bed and noticed the light still on in Liam's room. This was unusual because he usually had his music playing if he was still up. Everything was strangely quiet. I thought that he might have fallen asleep and forgotten about the light. I opened the door to find him hanging naked, above an overturned chair. Why? Why did he do it? Why did he do this to me?

Grace's teenage son had killed himself and she came to me to ask 'why'. The more Grace enquired about Liam and searched for answers the more everything pointed to that fact that Liam had been traumatised by bullying. The discovery that Liam had suffered alone and in silence for nearly two years, added to Grace's pain, guilt and sense of failure as a parent. 'Why didn't he tell me? I'm his mother. I love him. I could have helped him.'

No one knew of Liam's suffering and pain until it was too late. When Liam was 14 he loved athletics. He had no time for girls because he was too busy. A few boys started teasing him because he didn't have a girlfriend and he showed no interest in having one. It started as a joke trying to match Liam up with any and every girl they could think of. After a while the group decided he must be gay, and this became the focus of their fun. The fun turned into hostility as the rumours spread and more students became involved. Liam's depression and loneliness grew with every act of rejection, torment and innuendo.

Liam's suicide was not a spur of the moment thing. He had planned it very carefully. Liam had taken a saw from the shed and cut a very neat hole in the plaster ceiling exposing one of the beams. He had purchased a rope and gone to the trouble of learning how to make the perfect noose. He had made himself a banana sandwich which was found on his bedside table with one bite taken out of it. He chose a time when he knew his brother would be out, as he would be the one most likely to disturb him.

This heart-wrenching incident moved me deeply and set me on a mission of study, research and experimentation. I was determined to find ways to address the serious problems associated with bullying.

Liam's story is not an isolated one. In the 1990s a student in Sydney stood up in front of his class, looked every kid in the eye then shot himself in front of them. Why did he choose that class, those students, that time? What was he saying to those present?

Bullying has more victims than just the initial target. Some of the school shootings in America have been connected with acts of school bullying. At a recent training day we were informed that 70 young people commit suicide every year in Britain as a direct result of being bullied at school.[2]

People who have been seriously affected by bullying either turn inward on themselves, or lash out at others and the world. It has been reported that some perpetrators of horrific crimes have themselves been victims of bullying while at school. No one can ever truly know the impact that bullying may have had on the emotional and mental development of such people. However, we cannot ignore it or dismiss it lightly.

---

[2] Data supplied 2004 Babara Maines. I have been unable to obtain similar data relating to Australian schools.

An illustration of this ongoing effect was brought to my attention one morning. I was called out of a meeting at school to speak with a parent who had informed the office staff that I was needed urgently. This mother had driven nearly all the way to her place of employment that morning when she turned around and came directly to the school because of her concern for the safety and wellbeing of her daughter. Her daughter was going through some difficult experiences within her peer group, a situation that I was aware of. The girl's mother was distressed that her daughter was being bullied and might be unable to cope. As this mother spoke her emotional state deteriorated. 'I don't want my daughter to go through what I went through. I was bullied at school and I know how bad it can get.'

Her daughter was not being bullied at all.

There was definitely conflict between peers, but her daughter displayed all the social skills and confidence that she needed to keep her from becoming a victim. Unfortunately, this mother's own demons were being resurrected. What she believed may be happening to her daughter had re-opened old wounds that were hidden deep within herself. This mother was reliving the emotion, the fears and pain that had caused her so many traumas when she was at school many years ago. She was still a victim.

As part of my research, I undertook surveys with students and parents. The purpose of these surveys was to find out what people thought and felt, as well as gain an insight into what was really happening in our school. The surveys were anonymous and allowed the participants to speak up without fear of retribution. The response from parents, in particular, was overwhelming.

The stories they told of their children, as well as their own personal stories—some from 15–20 years ago—flowed forward as if they were experiencing them today. I occasionally thought I could see the stains of their tears on the paper. Many of these stories moved me greatly.

As a School Chaplain I found myself working more and more with students who were:
- experiencing social isolation,
- displaying signs of poor self-esteem,
- refusing to attend school,
- having regular outbursts of anger,
- displaying behaviour concerns,
- experiencing difficulties in making and keeping friends,
- unhappy or depressed.

Many of these students were suffering as a result of bullying. I was surprised at the extent to which bullying was the underlying cause for many of these problems.

Bullying is a serious problem and its impact can be severe. We need to re-visit the fundamental questions that schools, so far, have failed to address adequately.

- What is bullying?
- Why do students bully?
- Why are some people bullied while others are not?
- What can be done to assist those students who seem to be a target for every would-be bully around?
- What can be done to help those who, like Liam, suffer torment and pain silently every day?
- What can be done to combat bullying?
- What methods are more useful and effective in bringing about positive change in the behaviour of those who bully?
- What can be done to uncover what really is going on in our schools?

CHAPTER TWO

WHAT IS BULLYING?

If you can't hurt me, you can't bully me.

A colleague of mine, knowing of my interest in bullying, light-heartedly bumped into me in the staff room one morning.

'I'm going to bully you today,' he said standing in an aggressive manner.

'No you're not.'

'Yes I am.'

'No you're not.'

'Just watch me.'

'You can't bully me.'

'Why can't I?'

'Because bullying is about power and you don't have any power over me, so give it your best shot.'

I stood strongly with my head up looking him firmly in the eye.

'Well, I'll just have to find someone else to bully then,' he said, as he backed down and walked away.

This light-hearted, non-serious banter provides insight into understanding bullying. If schools are going to make inroads into beating bullying, it is important to have an understanding of what bullying is. Bullying is about power, it is the abuse of power. Students who are unable to hang on to or protect their power become victims.

Much can be achieved by teaching students how to use their power responsibly, and how to retain it when challenged. Having the ability to assertively respond to bullying behaviours determines whether a student will be a victim or not.

It is important to distinguish that 'bullying' and 'bullying behaviours' are different. Put simply, when the behaviours are hurtful and damaging, it *is* bullying. When they are not, it is not bullying. Bullying behaviour includes behaviour that does not constitute bullying. Bullying behaviour embraces both 'fun' and 'conflict'.

Most people would list the following behaviours as bullying:

- name calling

- pushing, punching
- making fun of others
- making threats
- rude comments
- making comments about a person's appearance
- mimicking
- interfering with another's property, and so on.

Most would agree that these behaviours are wrong, hurtful, and potentially damaging. In different circumstances, however, these same behaviours can be positive, friendly, bonding and relationship building. Many of us use these types of behaviour in a fun way with our friends every day. The ability to laugh and have fun with each other is important. If one of our friends does or says something silly or goofy, we will let them know all about it and get as much mileage out of it as we can. I actually find that those I don't poke fun at are the ones I don't know well, or I don't particularly like. The threats made against me by my colleague were relationship building. They brought us closer together and conveyed a message that I was fun, liked, accepted, and an OK guy to spend time with. We can hide each other's coffee cup, bump into each other in passing, point out to others the embarrassing things we each do, all in the name of fun. So when are these behaviours bullying, and when are they not?

Even when the intent is not to be friendly or nice, if the behaviour does not hurt the recipient, it is not 'bullying'. If you can't hurt me, you can't bully me. Here lies a clue in how to assist students to become 'bully-proof'. Bullying is about the impact it has on the recipient. Students can learn how to build and protect their sense of power. As illustrated in the previous chapter, the impact of bullying can be very serious and clearly the responsibility in overcoming bullying does not lie with the victim alone.

Bullying is theft. It is the stealing of a student's self-worth and power.

Bullies bully and wait for a reaction. The victim gets embarrassed, backs off, looks away or simply goes quiet as the bully steals a little power and grows in stature and social position. The more powerful the bully becomes, the weaker the victim becomes.

I often refer to this as a type of game where all students engage in a competition to accumulate power. All students are allocated 10 points of power. The game begins and the students start bustling for recognition and social position. The bullies look for those who may be vulnerable, sensitive and unable to protect their power. They fish. They bait their hooks with smart comments, insults, rude names, greasy threatening glares, and they look to recruit others who will support, acknowledge and join them. These followers encourage the bullies by laughing, mimicking, and joining in, which further contributes to the bullies' collection of power and feelings of importance. The followers are important to a bully, as they are needed not only to establish the bully's position, but also to retain his or her power, influence and control.

The bullies are constantly on the lookout for those who may be sensitive or reveal a weakness they can exploit. When students show signs that they are hurt, or demonstrate an inability to deflect or stand strong, they have really had some of their power points stolen from them. The bullies accumulate more power and the victim's power is further diminished. The victims start to feel isolated and rejected by the social-power group. In extreme cases the bullies end up wielding all the power and those who have been their victims struggle in isolation at the bottom of the social ladder . At the end of the game the bullies have accumulated more than their fair share of the power and their victims end up with little or no power at all. Bullying is a group thing. It operates on group dynamics and, in theory, has little to do with the person who is chosen as the victim. It is rare that a student bullies alone, but it occasionally does happen. Victims will often indicate that members of the group are different when on their own, or when away from their leader. Even the leaders have been known to be different when separated from the other group members. The group, and the power of the group, is defined by those outside the group. The group see those outside their group as different and not acceptable.

In the majority of bullying cases, the students engaging in the bullying have little or no feelings at all for their victims. They neither like nor dislike them. This insight has proven very powerful in getting bullying to stop. The bullying students simply use their victims as a means to establish and/or reinforce their social position and power within their own group setting. Most groups have one leader. The others in the group engage in bullying behaviours for different reasons.

Some do it to try and impress the leader and stay near the top of the power ladder. Some do it to keep safe. They feel it is far better to be a part of the power group than risk becoming one of their victims. Some students are bored and do not know how to have fun without hurting others. It means so much to young people to be a part of the popular group and some will do whatever it takes to get in and stay in.

Teachers often find it difficult to accurately identify bullying. This is understandable because playful fun, conflict, and bullying can all present with the same type of behaviours.

Conflict is not bullying

If two students are in a dispute and are roughly of equal power, it is not bullying. If students give as much as they get, it is not bullying. If the dispute is over a particular thing, it is unlikely to be bullying. Conflict issues should be managed by the school through peer mediation or other such programs.

Bullying occurs when there is an imbalance of power and that power is abused. Bullying is hurtful and ongoing. It is not a one-off incident. Bullying has the potential to cause deep emotional and psychological problems.

Shared responsibility is about beating and overcoming bullying.

After much research and experience I have arrived at what may appear to many as an overly simple conclusion: those who bully do so because they can, and those who are repeatedly subjected to bullying are bullied because they allow it.

CHAPTER THREE

BULLYING IS ALL ABOUT THE VICTIM

There was a lot of strong feeling. There were expressions of disgust, repulsion, abhorrence and anger.

It is not about the bullies

Traditionally schools have paid more attention to, and invested more time in, the bullies rather than the victims. When responding to bullying issues teachers have spent the majority of their time addressing and changing the behaviour of the bullies. In doing this, they overlook and neglect the students who are in the greater need of help. Even negative attention is better than no attention at all.

If the branch of a tree breaks the roof of your house, your first priority is to fix the roof. The problem tree can be looked at later. Why is it that schools want to fix the tree and ignore the roof? Traditionally schools have neglected 'victim impact' and concentrated on the bully.

Teachers have wasted a lot of time trying to solve 'bullying' problems—some of which have not been bullying at all. Victims have been given a paper and pen, instructed to write a statement of events and left alone. It is not unknown for teachers to act on accusations of bullying without having any contact with the victim at all. The teacher decides on the seriousness of the incident and the action that is to be taken based on information supplied, interpretation of the information, and their personal judgement, emotions, beliefs and values.

Teachers should make the 'victim' the priority, as well as the first and last point of call. This will save time and make positive inroads into stopping bullying.

Have you received details of an incident and thought 'this is nothing, it's no big deal,' or, 'Oh my goodness, he should be severely dealt with over this?'

It is not about what you think

Being human, our thoughts, instincts and opinions often influence our decision making. This can be a problem, particularly when it comes to responding to bullying. What you think is trivial, may in fact be causing severe distress to the victim, and what you think is serious, may in fact be having little impact, or causing no distress at all. Bullying is determined by the impact it is having on the victim.

Two totally separate incidents of bullying, reported to me by staff, illustrate how we interpret differently. Both reporting staff members were convinced that there was some serious bullying going on and expressed genuine concern for the targeted students. I arranged to meet the identified targets. They rejected the notion that they were being bullied. Both accepted that they had been involved in some playful activities and that these may have included some bullying behaviours. They insisted everybody was just mucking around and having fun and that they were happy at school and were not hurt or bothered by it. It was all in good fun, and they were engaging in it as well.

Neither showed any obvious signs of being a victim.

Denial can be a safety mechanism employed by victims who fear things will get worse if they speak up. I was careful to watch these students closely, even taking the opportunity to speak with one student's parents. It was important to identify any signs of unhappiness or symptoms that may indicate bullying. Everything supported the belief that the students were telling the truth.

I'm not suggesting that teachers should ignore 'bullying behaviour'; they most definitely should not. Teachers should respond to 'bullying behaviour' as they would any classroom management issue or they should talk privately with the suspected victim before making a referral.

To determine whether there is a genuine bullying issue, see the Is this Bullying? checklist in Appendix One. It provides a useful way to work through the issues.

It is not about how you feel

Humans are emotional beings. We react to injustice with anger. We react to sad events with tears and we experience all sorts of emotional reactions to all sorts of different stories and events. Our emotional reactions often impact on our thinking and influence our decision making. Do not allow your emotions to influence your responses to bullying.

At a recent training day on bullying, we were shown a video containing two bullying scenarios. (Both scenarios were taken from the television program 'Sticks and Stones'.) In groups we discussed what we would do and how we would address the bullying issues.

The first scenario involved a group of girls who were using put-downs and rude comments as a means of keeping an unwanted girl out of their group. There was a power imbalance of three to one. No matter how hard this one girl tried to get into the conversation and be nice, the other three took turns to come at her with rude, sarcastic, derogatory, put-down comments. There was no way they were going to accept this girl as an equal in their group. It was easy to identify the leader, as the other two were constantly looking to her for approval whenever they spoke. The three girls were having a good laugh at their victim's expense.

The second scenario portrayed two girls chasing and cornering another girl in an isolated area of the schoolyard. One of the bullying girls was physical and very aggressive. She demeaned her victim by standing in her face and demanding she apologise for, what she said were 'poor manners'. The victim stood weakly with her head down staring at the ground. She reluctantly and fearfully apologised, but that was not good enough for her power-hungry assailant. This bully demanded that her victim get down on her knees and apologise properly. The bully was being supported, encouraged, and egged on by an accomplice who was mimicking every order that the other bully barked. The victim was pushed to her knees where she apologised for a second time. 'Louder, I said louder.' The victim had a can of Coke in her hand that she had just opened and commenced to drink. The bully snatched the can from her, spat in it and demanded that she drink it. 'Drink it! Drink it! I said drink it!' The helpless victim knelt in silent refusal. The bully grabbed her, pushed her to the ground and proceeded to make her drink by forcing the can into her mouth. With this the contents of the can spilled all over the girl's face and onto her hair.

In groups we discussed what we would do about both scenarios. The different responses were interesting. Most people felt the second scenario was much more serious than the first. Calling the police, suspending the bullies, immediately removing the bullies from the school to ensure the victim's safety, were among the suggested responses. There was a lot of strong feeling. There were expressions of disgust, repulsion, abhorrence and anger. There were demands for justice by immediate intervention and punishment. Even though this was only a training scenario people found it difficult to control the emotions that were driving their thinking. There were a number of red faces and clenched fists. This scenario had obviously touched some raw nerves.

Things were much calmer when discussing the first scenario. Most thought that talking privately to the girls in an off-the-record sort of way would be the most appropriate way to respond and deal with the situation. No one expressed any real concern for the victim. Most thought the bullying was cruel, not nice and should not be allowed to continue, but it was no big deal in comparison.

Which bullying scenario is most likely to cause the greater harm to the victim? Of course, the answer lies with the victim. It was interesting that all the suggestions gave time and attention to the bullies, all the focus was on them. What about the victims, where were they in all this? I thought that both situations should be handled in the same manner.

In the first scenario, the victim was facing rejection and social isolation. Research, as well as personal experience, has confirmed that this type of bullying has more potential to cause serious psychological and emotional problems than the other. The first example of bullying is more likely to result in long-term problems such as school refusal, low self-esteem, depression and self-harm.

In the second scenario, even though the victim was, at the time in a more revolting and physically dangerous situation, there was more she could do to keep safe in the future. In this scenario the girl's attackers were not her friends or her social support. She did not need or rely on them for anything. It would be easy for her to avoid her attackers and draw on the support and comfort of her friends.

The true impact or the level of seriousness of the bullying can only be determined by working with the victims. Bullying is not about you, what you think or what you feel. It is not about the bully either. Always assess bullying based on the impact it is having on the victims. Bullying is all about the victims.

The impact and the effects that bullying has on an individual varies from student to student. The effect can range from simple annoyance and frustration through to anger, defiance, withdrawal, school refusing, physical and psychiatric illness, depression, self-hatred and self-harm.

All bullying can be effectively dealt with by using the same method regardless of personal feelings or perceived degree of seriousness. The impact and the effects that bullying has had on a recipient should have no bearing at all on how you respond to the bullying. It will, however, have some bearing on what follow-up support is offered.

CHAPTER FOUR
KIM'S STORY

If it continues, tell the teacher.

'I had only been in secondary school two days before I was pushed, kicked, insulted and had my books and things thrown on the ground.' After just two days in her new school, Kim found herself being tormented and bullied by a boy in her class who she had never met or known before. She had experienced a little bit of bullying in primary school but nothing quite like this. Kim had been allocated a locker above Ben's. Without warning or consideration, Kim suddenly found herself being recklessly pushed aside so Ben could have the space he obviously believed was his right.

Kim tried to stand her ground and found she was repeatedly subjected to rude names and derogatory remarks about her appearance in the presence of her new peer group. Some of the other students responded in a way that encouraged Ben to continue his efforts of hurtful, aggressive behaviours.

Ben was trying very hard to create an image and make a name for himself. He acted tough and was trying to be funny, cool, and make others he considered nobodies fear him. He wanted to impress and be in control.

For Kim this was the beginning of an ongoing, concentrated, cruel assault. It wasn't long before Kim became distressed and fearful in her new school environment. Within two days Kim had lost confidence and became fearful of her tormentor as well as going to her locker. In class, the very presence of this boy and his constant loud aggressive manner caused Kim to squirm and want to escape.

Later that day when she arrived home, Kim found herself sobbing uncontrollably as she tried to explain to her parents what was happening at school. She didn't want to return to school the next day but her father insisted that she needed to be strong and not let one boy upset her.

Kim reluctantly and fearfully returned to school, holding on to what her parents had told her. 'If it continues, tell the teacher.' Ben wasted no time in picking up where he left off. He continued to treat Kim in ways that further contributed to her escalating distress and feelings of helplessness. She didn't want to tell the teacher but in the end, in fear and trembling, not knowing what else to do, she tearfully and nervously confided in her new home group teacher. The teacher was well aware of the school policy and procedures in dealing with bullying. The teacher documented the incident and discussed the matter with both the coordinator and myself. We then set the wheels in motion. Kim was cared for and praised for her courage to speak up. Kim told her sad story. She revealed feelings of fear, hurt, humiliation and wanting the bullying to stop. The *shared responsibility* method was explained and her permission sought to follow it.

Kim expressed real concern about returning to her class. What will the other students think of her? What will she say when they ask her where she has been? What if Ben and the others pick on her even more for dobbing? What if she starts crying again?

In preparing Kim for her return to class, I pointed out the importance of courage and looking strong and happy, even if she didn't feel that way. I talked with her about how the other students might react if she walked into class with her head down, looking hurt, wounded and upset. Kim understood that this would not be helpful. I talked with her about how they might react if she walked in with her head up, looking strong, happy and energetic. No one needed to know where she had been, or why. Kim had been called to the office. There are many reasons why a student could be called to the office. Kim could see the difference her body language would make to her return. We practised ways of presenting with strong body language—keeping her head up, standing with big shoulders, using her eyes and natural bubbly personality to cover up her wounded spirit. She acknowledged that we can't change the behaviour of others, but we can and must take control of our own. Kim learnt quickly and was being empowered with every short exercise and instruction. We practised what she could say and how she should say it. I pointed out to Kim that the boy who had been bullying her would be called out of class shortly after she returned. Kim was nervous but agreed to share the responsibility with us in bringing about her safety and stopping the bullying. Kim left with a lot more confidence and control than she displayed when she arrived.

I found out the next day from Kim what she did and how she felt.

> When I was walking back to class I had butterflies in my stomach. I didn't want to go but I knew I had to. I was determined to look strong so I took a few deep breaths, lifted my head and went for it. When I got to the classroom, the door was locked. I knocked and

called out to the kids inside to let me in. I turned it into a little joke and demanded they open the door. The kids in the class were expecting me to be upset, but I wasn't. I immediately asked what they were doing and what I needed to do to catch up. Mr Findley had prepared me for their questions.

'Are you all right?'

'Where have you been?'

I just told them I had to go to the office.

'What for?'

'I just had to go to the office that's all, it's no big deal.'

I was surprised how easily it came out and how confident I sounded. I was feeling like myself. I like to have fun and to laugh and talk a lot. In a very short time I was really feeling happy and not just pretending. Ben said nothing. I think he was surprised that I was happy and energetic. About five minutes later a note came from the office and he was taken out. I just continued to be myself. When Ben returned to class about thirty minutes later, he was very quiet. He didn't say or do anything to me. I thought this was rather strange. He was quiet but he didn't appear upset. I really didn't see him much for the rest of the day. When I went to my locker he wasn't around. I went home and explained to my parents what had happened. Mr Findley told me that he would talk to me again the next day. Mum said that she would like to be there but I didn't know what time he would call me. Mr Findley told me that Mum could ring and talk to him at any time. The next morning I actually wanted to go to school. I wasn't scared at all. When I arrived at school Ben was a different boy. He not only wasn't bullying me, he was actually being nice. He stood back at the lockers and waited until I and others had finished. When a girl tried to hurry me up he actually told her to be patient and wait. All the kids in the class noticed a big change. People started to whisper and ask,

'What's happened to Ben? He's different.'

Ben's whole attitude to everybody had changed. I don't know what Mr Findley said to him, but whatever it was it worked. Mr Findley called me out of class towards the end of the day. I was happy, very happy. Things had changed a lot in one day. Ben had not only stopped bullying he was being friendly and nice. He came up to me when I was working on a computer and asked what I was doing. Everyone likes the new Ben a lot better.

The change in Kim and Ben was remarkable. Kim expressed feeling happy and safe at school. Her body language and confidence had improved over 200 per cent in one day. I spent a little more time with her debriefing the situation and giving her some ideas on how to become more bully proof. Kim was a delight to work with. I remember telling her that she was number twenty-six on my list of consecutive positive results in beating bullying using this method. Ben also was a delight to work with. He shared in the responsibility of finding a solution. Both these students learnt from this experience.[3]

---

[3] See Chapter 6 for the *shared responsibility* method outline.

CHAPTER FIVE

ASSESSING THE IMPACT

A real person with real feelings.

When supporting a student who has been the recipient of bullying, be aware of the need to respond to the issue on two fronts. On one front, you will support the student and deal with the bullying issue. On the other front, you will consider and plan any ongoing support the student may need to equip them for their return and survival in the school community. Always begin by caring for the victim, provide the needed support as well as working on what needs to be done to stop the bullying. The need for long-term or further support can be discussed and planned later or it will arise naturally as you work through the process. It is important that the student feels supported and knows that you are with them, sharing the responsibility in finding a solution and putting a stop to the bullying.

Pay careful attention to identifying any natural skills and abilities the recipient may possess that could be helpful in dealing and coping with the situation. Take particular notice of the way the recipient presents to you. Reading body language is important in assessing the impact of bullying. This type of assessment is not difficult and will come naturally to most people.

Take note of the following:
- The level of confidence the student displays.
  - Does the student appear timid, embarrassed or scared?
- The degree of eye contact the student makes when they speak to you.
  - Does the student just sit there staring at the floor?
- The way the student walks and moves.
  - Does the student walk with small steps, head down and shoulders stooped?
- The manner in which the student speaks. Does the student:
  - speak quietly, hesitantly, with a weak tone?
  - express opinions confidently?
  - have the confidence and courage to speak up for themselves?

- The degree of power and control the student may have.
  - Does the student know what they want?
  - Has the student tried ways of dealing with the situation on their own?
  - Does the student have any meaningful level of peer support?
- The emotional state of the student.
  - Is the student angry, fearful or badly scarred?
  - Is the student depressed?
  - Can the student bounce back and recover quickly?
  - Will the student easily re-establish any lost confidence or self-esteem?

After making this assessment, concentrate on providing the needed support and what needs to be done to stop the bullying. As stated earlier, the need for long-term or further support can be addressed later. What is needed now is that the bullying be stopped.

As the support person you need to:

- convince the student that you are on their side and that you now share the ownership of the problem and will follow the matter through to the desired end,
- quell any fears the student may have by assuring them that you won't make things worse for them,
- assure them you will not act without their knowledge or permission,
- state clearly that your aim is to help them to be safe and feel safe, and to stop the bullying.

Getting the story isn't all that important even though in the past it appears to be what has driven school procedures. In beating or stopping bullying the story itself is of little value, other than knowing what has happened so a record of the incident can be kept on file.

'Bill reported that he was being bullied by Sam,' is really sufficient for the school records. However, I do suggest a little more detail be included as outlined in the Shared Responsibility Meeting Form (see Appendix One). What is important is that it be recorded, 'Bill reported it' and that the school has responded.

What is of most importance is the recipient. Bullying is all about the recipient. How is this student feeling and coping with the situation? What impact is the bullying having on them? What needs to be done to help this student to be safe and feel safe?

Empathic statements such as 'I can understand how that would upset you' validate feelings and help the recipient feel supported and understood. Be an active listener. Draw out feelings and note the effects the bullying is having. Be sympathetic to emotions and be careful not to make judgement statements such as, 'He should never have done that', 'I can't believe that anyone could do such a thing' or 'We must make sure they don't get away with this type of behaviour'.

Telling their story, even though it is of little value in solving the bullying problem, can be extremely important to the student who has been the subject of bullying. They need to be listened to, heard, believed, and have the opportunity to talk. They should not be cross-examined, or asked what they have done to cause this. Sometimes it is useful to ask how and when it all started. Notes should be taken for the records but not as the main objective of the meeting. I suggest that you write it up later or take down dot points so all your attention can be directed to supporting the bullied student. Questions such as 'What are they doing?' may be useful but not as useful as 'How is all this making you feel?' or 'What impact is this having on you?'

Where possible, use open-ended questions to stimulate discussion. 'I've noticed that you are going through a hard time and have been unhappy at school lately, what are you doing to manage?' and 'A teacher reported seeing some students giving you a hard time, how is this affecting you?'

The story will come out naturally as you encourage the students to talk in an atmosphere of care, safety and support. Even if you suspect that the total truth is not being told, getting to the truth is not the objective. The objective is to support the recipient, help them to be safe and to feel safe, and to put a stop to the bullying.

It is important to explain what *shared responsibility* means to the students so they can understand and have confidence in the method.

Explain that:

- you *will* invite the student/s who are bullying in for a talk as a group (or individually).
- They, the recipient, *will not* be a part of this discussion.
- the group *will not* be accused of anything. They are not in trouble, and will simply be asked to share the responsibility in helping solve the problem.
- you will be taking an impact statement from them, the recipient, and with their permission, share it with the bullying group.
- the purpose of the impact statement is to help the bullying student/s realise what they are doing, and how their actions are impacting on and affecting the recipient.
- the group will be asked what they are prepared to do to help, and what they decide will be written down and kept on file.
- because of this approach it is unlikely the group will get angry and things get worse for them.
- the *shared responsibility* method has been very effective and powerful in stopping bullying.

Ask the recipient what it is they would like to happen. In most cases they will respond by saying 'I just want the bullying to stop.' Remind the recipient that you share their thoughts and your aim is to help them to be safe and feel safe, as well as stop the bullying. It is important that the recipient understands that you *will not* be trying to keep their identity a secret.

Seek a commitment and permission to act from the recipient. It is important in establishing trust that the student knows and understands that you will not act without their knowledge or permission. Ask what they think about the process. If the student is hesitant or non-committal, outline other ways that may be employed to deal with the problem. These may include mediation, ignoring it, or getting assistance in developing skills and responses that may result in them dealing with the situation without involving others. Most students are happy to give *shared responsibility* a try. Being a recipient of bullying often brings with it feelings of having little or no control over what is happening, The *shared responsibility* approach is valuable in assisting the student to take ownership of the problem without feeling they are in it alone. It is empowering for the student to know that their thoughts, feelings and opinions are being considered and that they are in control without having to shoulder the full responsibility.

Upon gaining permission, seek the names of all those involved in the group, even those on the fringe who don't necessarily engage in the bullying themselves. These people can be important in using group dynamics to bring about the desired change in behaviour. When a group is larger that five or six, it becomes more of a challenge to manage, but I have worked effectively with seven. Sometimes only one student is named as engaging in the bullying. This is rare but the *shared responsibility* method has proven to be just as effective working with one student as it has with groups. It is not important to know or push for names any earlier. *Who* is not as important as *what*. *What* is not as important as the impact on, and the feelings of, the recipient.

I can remember working with a student who was determined that under no circumstances would he let the names of his tormentors slip. After going through the whole support process including the taking of an impact statement, he realised that nothing further could be accomplished without me knowing who they were. 'I suppose I better tell you who they are,' he said. Unknown to him I already knew who they were, but I felt it important not to put him under any more unnecessary pressure. He was listened to, cared for, supported and, in the end, empowered to act.

Prepare the recipients for the ways in which the members of the bullying group may decide to assist.

The bullying students may decide to:
- apologise,
- approach the recipient and explain that they were only having fun and didn't mean to upset them,
- let the recipient know that there is no reason to be afraid and they won't bully them any more,
- just leave them alone by not saying or doing anything.

If the recipients are prepared for the bullies' responses, they are less likely to freak out if approached by members of the group.

Take an impact statement from the recipient that explains how they are feeling and what impact the bullying has had on them. This statement will be shared with the bullying students during the *shared responsibility* meeting. The impact statement is designed to:

• help the members of bullying group reflect on what they are doing so they can see how their actions and behaviour are impacting on, and hurting, their target.

• get the bullying students to feel empathy for their victim. Often students engage in bullying activities without considering how the recipient may be feeling or how they may be hurt.

• help the members of the bullying group realise that their object of fun or torment is a real person with real feelings.

It is believed that children from around the age of six or seven develop the ability to feel outside themselves. They can cry, feel sad, and respond to the pain, hurt and emotions of others.

Spend some time getting the impact statement from the recipient. Make sure you appear more interested in the student than the statement. You can either get the student to write about how they feel or, as I do, take down points throughout the session that reflect their feelings and the impact the bullying is having on them. Respond to their story in ways that will help the recipient feel you are listening, you care and you understand. Read the impact statement back to the student and ask if there is anything in it they feel uncomfortable with the group knowing. Be sensitive to this. Use wisdom and your professional judgement in leaving out personal details that may be embarrassing, even if the student doesn't request it. An impact statement may read something like this:

> I have been sad and unhappy at school for about a month now. I feel that nobody likes me and I'm on my own all the time. They all make fun of me and make me feel left out and that they don't want me around. I don't fit in here any more. I tried convincing mum I was sick so I didn't have to come to school but she made me come, so I ran away and wagged. We had a fight because I want to go to a different school, but she said I can't. I've been crying a lot and having bad dreams. I hate school. I'm scared to go the toilet at school and to my locker. I'm starting to think that there is something seriously wrong with me. I don't know what I've done to make everybody hate me.

Some students, particularly younger ones, may find it easier to draw a picture indicating how they feel and this could be used in the group to discuss and draw out just how they might be feeling.

During the *shared responsibility* meeting you can either read the impact statement or convey it in your own words for emphasis. Avoid wording the statements in a way that attributes blame or includes nasty incidents that may point to a particular person. Concentrate on the feelings and the impact points, rather than the incidents. Note that in the above statement there is no reference to what the group has been doing. When students write their own statements they often include names and incidents. The purpose of the statement may need to be explained further and some guidance and editing may be required.

In addition, the sharing of other stories where people have been seriously affected or hurt by bullying should be used for establishing empathy. The potential impact of these statements should not be underestimated. This will be further expanded in Chapter 6 which deals with the *shared responsibility* meeting.

Statements containing details and incidents of bullying can be placed on file but are not useful or important in beating bullying using the *shared responsibility* method. If you decide to record and file such details it is important to realise that this information must be made available to the student and their family upon request. All teacher records, notes and files on a student can be requested and used in a department or school enquiry. If you feel the need to record the incident details, do so in a manner that does not imply judgement. 'Bill reported that he was being hit, kicked, punched and bullied by Ben', is better than, 'Ben was involved in hitting, kicking, punching and bullying Bill.'

Inform the recipient of your time frame and limitations. Because of other responsibilities it may not be possible for you to act on the bullying problem immediately. Inform the recipient that it may take you a few days to get things moving. Provide the recipient with a few basic strategies that will help them avoid the group and stay safe until you can catch up with those implicated in the bullying. Inform the recipient that you will be following up with them after the meeting, and then again a number of times over the following few weeks. Get a commitment from the recipient to share the responsibility and report any further incidents of bullying immediately. Now the wheels have begun to turn it is important that things are followed through to the desired end. If the recipient is in need of further or ongoing support make another appointment to discuss and plan it. Sometimes it is appropriate and useful in empowering the recipient with some positive body language skills during this first session. For more information on this refer to Chapter 14 on Body Language.

CHAPTER SIX

THE SHARED RESPONSIBILITY MEETING

I've called you together today to seek your assistance in finding a solution to a problem.

This chapter outlines the steps to be followed in the *shared responsibility* meeting:

- welcome the students,
- introduce the impact statement,
- teach the students about bullying,
- discuss impact part two,
- seek a commitment,
- outline the school policy, procedures and legal requirements,
- outline the school's follow-up process,
- conclude the meeting.

Invite all the students who have been named as belonging to the group involved in bullying behaviour to a meeting. As mentioned in the last chapter, sometimes the recipient only identifies one student as the bully. This is rare but the *shared responsibility* meeting as outlined here is just as effective working with one student as it is with a group. Of course, only working with one student eliminates any use of group dynamics but the impact statement and the concentration on establishing empathy is of more importance and power. It is important that this meeting be conducted in a relaxed non-threatening manner because the purpose of the meeting is to seek the assistance and cooperation of the students to share the responsibility of finding a solution to the problem.

Welcome

Make the meeting room as safe and as friendly as possible. Welcome the group and thank them for coming. Explain why you have called them together. A welcome might go like this:

Thanks for coming. The reason I have called you together today is to seek your assistance in finding a solution to a problem that I have recently become aware of. I want to make it clear that you are not in trouble and you are not being blamed for anything. As a school community there are sometimes issues that arise that emphasise the need to work together and share the responsibility in making our school a safe and better place for everyone.

The other day I was asked to speak with (Name) who, I found out, has been going through a rough time at school lately. In speaking with (Name) I discovered that the problem has something to do with this group. I want to emphasise again that this is not about trouble or blame. I know there are always two sides to every story. What I would like to do is talk with you about how we might work together in finding a solution and avoiding potential trouble if we can.

People tend to become defensive, uncomfortable and uncooperative if they feel they are being accused or blamed. Even though you are fairly sure that they have been behaving irresponsibly, this tactic is subconsciously stating that you are on to them but are giving them an opportunity to put things right so trouble can be avoided. Most students will want to avoid trouble if they can. This approach is also modelling and teaching a constructive method of dealing with and responding to conflict. It is also empowering and engaging, as it endeavours to share the responsibility for what is happening among all those involved. It has the potential to make the students feel that they are valued as important, intelligent and responsible members of the school community and therefore should have input into what is happening and what can happen in their school. Many of these students have real leadership potential. An added benefit to the meeting is that it can provide an opportunity to build positive relationships with students that other staff may have had difficulty reaching.

Ask the group if they were aware of any problem, or if they had noticed that the recipient has been unhappy lately. Let them talk if they want to, even if their intention is to try to justify their treatment of the victim. There are often reasons or events that lie at the root of some of these situations. Listen to the group and affirm their feelings where appropriate.

It is not important to establish the facts or get the whole story, but it may be important for them to be heard if they feel the need to share their views on what has happened. Be careful not to pass judgement or take sides.

At the appropriate time express your concern for (Name).

Impact statement

Introduce the impact statement or picture. Over time I have preferred to pick out the feeling and impact words from the recipient's statement and put them across in my own words. I have found that it presents naturally and has potentially greater impact. It also allows me to keep a better connection with the group and observe their responses and their body language.

It might be presented something like this:

> It's not a good thing to feel *not liked, unwanted* and *left out*. In speaking with (Name) I found out that whatever it is that's happening here at school is making it *difficult for him/her to be happy and fit in*. He/she expressed a *fear of going to the lockers and the toilets*. He/she was even talking about *running away and changing schools*. (Name) told me that he/she is *feeling sad and lonely* and that he/she *feels that everybody hates him/her*. I found one very unhappy person. I don't like it when any of our students feel this way. (Name) also told me that he/she has been having *trouble sleeping* and is starting to think there is something *seriously wrong with him/her*.

The words in italics are those gleaned from the impact statement taken during the time I spent with the recipient. To aid impact I presented them in a story using my words.

Teach

Teach the students what bullying is and the potential damage and impact it can have on some people. This section is important and should be introduced with these questions:
- Is bullying a good or a bad thing?
- Do you understand what bullying is and the effect it can have on some people?

Sometimes presenting a short list of typical bullying behaviours such as name calling, making threats or deliberately leaving someone out is a good way to start things off. Ask the group the question, Are these things bullying? When working with individuals, I sometimes get the student to complete a written survey before discussing it with them (see Appendix One for the 'What is Bullying?' survey sheet).

The survey lists a number of bullying behaviours and poses the question, Is this bullying? It also includes a scale from 1–10 to register the impact these behaviours may have on a recipient. These survey results give an indication of a student's sense of social responsibility as well as leading into the discussion of the topic.

Remember, bullying is *all* about the person it is happening to. Also remember that bullying behaviour can be negative and hurtful, as well as positive and bonding. Nearly all the bullying behaviour you can think of will have both positive and negative potential depending on the circumstances in which it occurs, its intent, and the manner in which the recipient interprets and receives it. An example is name calling. I have a mate who calls me 'Finders' and I also have a name for him. Neither of these names are the names our parents gave us. Occasionally, he might refer to me as 'boofhead'. To us this is a sense of fun and bonding. It is not intended to be rude or hurtful and it is not. It is name calling but it's not bullying. You might be thinking, when is something like making threats not bullying? It doesn't take much to recall a playful incident after which someone will say 'I'll kill you for that'. Again, in such a circumstance, this is not bullying.

Stimulate a discussion around whether a behaviour is bullying or whether it is not. You will need to think on your feet and work with what you are given and what you can feed in. If the students show any signs of becoming defensive, reassure them that this is not about trouble or blame; it is about working together, and sharing the responsibility in helping to find a solution.

Most students have no idea of the potential serious consequences that bullying can have on some people. Take the opportunity to teach them.

Impact part two

Storytelling has always been a powerful teaching tool. Share some stories that you have encountered, have heard or read about, where bullying has caused serious problems for the recipient. Be careful not to use examples that are close to home. Stories from your own experience, when you were at school, previous schools, news items, people you have met, or even some of the stories I have included in this book, may be helpful. Do not underestimate the power of these impact stories in connecting to young people.

An extremely challenging student was referred to me by his coordinator. This boy was engaging in extreme physical and violent bullying. He was in constant trouble, did not respect or fear any type of authority, and had been suspended a number of times for acts of fighting and violence at school. He had also been in trouble with the police over similar incidents outside the school. The coordinator referred him to me with the words, 'This will be your greatest challenge yet!'

I knew of this boy and had tried to connect with him about a year earlier with limited success. To make things even more challenging, the coordinator had met with the boy earlier and informed him that he had to go through the school bullying system and I would be talking with him. He had time to prepare and he knew what I would be talking with him about. I spent time with his victim and went through all the support procedures that are outlined in the previous chapter. I obtained permission from the student to speak to his tormentor and implement the *shared responsibility* method.

I had to wait a day for him to return from a suspension. The boy arrived at my office in a defensive uncooperative mood. I started trying to be friendly and asking him to relax. I explained that he wasn't in trouble and I just wanted his help in solving a problem. He interrupted by saying he knew exactly why he was with me and he was not going to help or cooperate in any way. He said he hated this kid and believed he deserved everything he was giving him. He adamantly stated that he didn't care if he got suspended again and he wasn't finished with this kid yet. I shared his victim's impact statement, and he laughed. He appeared pleased and gloated over his victim's expressions of fear and distress.

When I finished he simply smiled and said 'good'. I listened to him outline what he thought of his victim and why he felt like he did. I didn't judge or condemn, I simply listened and showed an interest in what he was saying. I continued with the process, asking him if bullying was good or bad. He responded by saying it was bad. A discussion took place about why he believed it was bad. The discussion developed to the point where we found ourselves talking about those who had been seriously affected by bullying. I shared the story of how and why I got interested in bullying. I told him the story of the boy who was found hanged as a result of bullying and the distressed mother. This boy was noticeably moved. I shared a few more stories of others who had lashed out and hurt others as a result of being bullied. I told him that bullying was a serious matter with serious consequences for some people. The boy started to ask questions and his defensiveness disappeared. I asked if he was willing to help me solve the problem and what was he prepared to do to help.

Without hesitation he outlined what he would do, which included leaving the victim alone and ceasing the bullying. I went through the school policy and procedures about second offenders, but I knew that the fear of consequences would not be a factor in his decision. He started to tell me stories and to open up. He initiated a discussion on the fact that no one could control him. I agreed with him that no one could control him and challenged him to consider if he had control of himself. The boy thought deeply and replied, 'I lose it, even mum can't control or stop me.'

I said, 'Can you control yourself? You need to.' I empathised with him and his feeling that the whole world was against him, and I felt that I had made a friend. He told me that no one ever listens to him or talked with him nicely. No one had ever talked to him like this before.

'If it helps maybe we should do it again.' I didn't want to push it and I couldn't really see him taking up my offer. Ten minutes later he was in the middle of a fight in the schoolyard. The teachers could not control him and he wasn't listening or following any instructions. A teacher, knowing that he had recently been with me, came and got me. I initially thought that he had taken me for a ride and gone after his victim. He would not talk or respond to any teacher who tried to calm him down or get him out of the yard. When I arrived he was standing in an aggressive manner, his mouth clenched tightly. He looked at me and said, 'Hi Sir.'

I told him that I had heard that he was angry and asked if it had anything to do with what we had discussed earlier. He explained that he had made many enemies and this kid just came after him, he had been after him for a while. He had to defend himself. At the time of writing this story he has not bullied again to my knowledge. I caught up with his victim two and three times a day for a week. Numerous follow-ups indicated that he was safe, felt safe and the bullying had stopped.

Do not underestimate the power of impact stories in getting empathy and changing bullying behaviour. The victim's impact statement meant nothing, but the other stories connected strongly. This all took under half an hour. It was a powerful, moving experience. This boy's response and his dramatic change caused an emotional response in me.

Be careful not to leave the bullying students with the impression that their target is at risk of self-harm. Victims can learn to cope and effectively deal with bullying behaviour with support. In one such group meeting, a student commented, 'Oh my God, she's not going to kill herself, is she?' Take time to reassure the students that this is not the case. However, the students must understand that the potential impact of bullying should not be underestimated nor taken for granted.

It is our responsibility to teach our students about their behaviour and the possible consequences of it. We have a responsibility to teach them about what bullying is and is not, as a part of values education. I believe that such teaching adds to the impact and calls for a responsible approach from the students. If a student goes through a process where they are simply requested to assist in solving someone else's problem without learning about bullying and its potential dangers, then they are more likely to miss the point and bully again.

Commitment

Seek a commitment by asking the students what they are prepared to do to help solve the problem. You might start by saying: 'As I explained earlier, I have brought you together to ask you to help me solve a problem. Now I want you to think what you can do to help.' Take brief notes of any suggestions or commitments so you can complete your paper work later. Thank them for their ideas. You could affirm their ideas with comments such as:

- That will help, that's a great idea, thank you. What about you (Name)?
- If you would do that, it will go a long way in solving the problem. Thank you. Can I write that down? I really think that will help.

School policy, procedure and legal requirements

Explain the school policy, procedure and legal requirements to the group and explain that you are required to keep a record of the meeting. For example, you may explain like this:

> It's important that you all know that I'm required by the school and the law to make a record of this meeting and to keep it on file. It's a simple record of who was here, the time and date we met, what it was about, and the outcome.

> The concern or the statement that I shared with you earlier about how (Name) is feeling at the moment will be part of this. The form requires me to indicate if you have been cooperative or uncooperative in helping to solve the problem, and I would like to thank you all for being so helpful and cooperative. I have been really impressed. I have written down what you are prepared to do to help, and if you follow through that will be the end of the matter. I'll read it back to you so you can check to see if I've got it right. If I haven't, I'll change it.

Read back what they have indicated and alter it if necessary.

Outline of the school's follow-up process

Outline the school's disciplinary process in dealing with bullying. You could explain it like this:

> You need to know that if there are any further incidents of this type, it will be considered a second incident. With a second

incident the school may require the coordinators (disciplinary staff) be involved and most likely there will be consequences. If this happens it is not the end of the world. We will talk with you again about whatever it is that has happened. We are interested in your story and we will not be jumping to any conclusions. However, the school will look upon a second incident more seriously.

If there are further incidents of this type, the school will need to involve your parents. There will be further consequences and we will need to look more seriously as to why this is continuing to happen. This is another reason why the school keeps these records as it helps us identify those students who are having difficulty mixing positively with other students. Some students need help in learning how to exist positively in a school community.

In the end, if a student continues to bully and threaten the safety of others, they may be asked to consider another school. To my knowledge this has never happened. It never gets that far.

Conclude the meeting by communicating to the group that you appreciate their help and if the problem is solved they will hear no more about it. Ask for questions and enquire as to how they are feeling about what has happened and the process. You may close the meeting like this:

Thank you all for your help and ideas. If we all work together and share the responsibility, I'm confident the problem will be solved and it will all be behind us.

How are you people feeling about the situation and the process?

Do you feel that it is fair?

Does anyone have any questions or any final thing you would like to say before you go back to class?

I will most probably catch up with each of you individually in about a week to see how things are going and how you are feeling about it all. I will also keep in touch with (Name) just to make sure he/she is OK. Well, thanks again for your help. I will see you around.

It is important that you make it known to the group that you will be following things up with the recipient and also with them.

Follow up at decreasing levels of frequency for about three weeks. The majority of follow-ups will be with the recipient. The first follow-up should take place the day after the *shared responsibility* meeting. Further follow-ups should take place on a daily basis for three or four days and then decrease in the second and third week. This is not as time consuming as it may first appear. These students can be spoken to just in passing in the schoolyard, at roll call, or briefly between classes. You can even arrange for the student to call in to see you briefly every recess or lunchtime for a few days. The time required for each follow-up will decrease, and after the first couple of times it can be as quick as five seconds. One student required about one minute on the first follow-up and over the next three weeks when he saw me coming he just gave me a 'thumbs up' signal. In following up with a victim you need to enquire about their feelings of safety and if things are OK.

One week after the *shared responsibility* meeting a quick follow-up with the bullies (individually) should take place. Enquire how things went in helping to fix the problem, and how things are going now. Thank them again for their cooperation and help. This will remind them that the school has not forgotten and is following through with the issue.

It is fairly uncommon that the process ever goes beyond the first *shared responsibility* meeting. A second meeting has been required in a few instances but has rarely involved the same victim.

Parent involvement has rarely been needed but is essential where more complex problems may be uncovered and further team support may be needed in caring for and working with the bullying student. The need to suggest that a student who continues to bully be asked to find another school is also rare. In my experience the need to take things this far has never arisen. However, I believe that including this as a part of the school policy and procedures can, and does, act as a positive deterrent. Schools need to draw up policy and procedures sometimes speculating on what may happen and how they will respond if a situation arises. Schools need to communicate to their community that all students are cared for and that student safety and wellbeing is of the highest priority.

Note that the emphasis is primarily on the welfare of all students and the aim is to ensure student safety and bring about positive change in bullying behaviour. It is not about punishment, revenge or even justice. In stating this, it must be emphasised that school bullying will not be tolerated.

CHAPTER SEVEN

HANG IN THERE!

I had had enough of their justification, light-hearted, non-serious, 'this is a joke' type responses and attitudes.

Facilitating a *shared responsibility* meeting can give rise to all sorts of powerful, personal emotions. These emotions can be challenging and as different as the faces of the students involved in each meeting. In the time I have been using the *shared responsibility* method I have experienced many emotions including feelings of:
- elation,
- joy and excitement,
- pride and achievement,
- disappointment and doubt,
- failure and discouragement,
- nervousness and caution,
- anger and frustration.

There have also been the times when I have been so deeply moved and touched by a student's empathy and response that I found myself fighting back the tears that were welling up in my eyes. Some emotions have the potential to cause a facilitator to consider changing tack and attempting to deal with the bullying issue another way. Do not become a victim of your feelings by responding to such emotions, particularly the negative ones.

During the developmental stages of the *shared responsibility* method, I have experimented with a number of settings, theories and ideas that may be helpful in beating bullying. As you would expect, I found that some were more helpful and useful than others. The use of impact statements and stories with their appeal for empathy in particular, raised some serious doubts and concerns within me. Unexpectedly, I was faced with the need to deal with some negative emotions in myself. Sometimes the initial student reaction and response left me feeling disillusioned, downhearted, frustrated and wanting to give up or change tack. What I learnt over time was not to give up and become a victim of my own emotional reactions. I discovered that the facilitator's emotions have little or no bearing at all on the outcome, unless of course, they cause a person to succumb to the temptation to abandon or divert from the method.

My first group meeting was rather large, a group of seven. The bullied person was socially on the fringe of her group and inadvertently made a comment about another person to a group member. This group member was sensitive to the comment, and in a very short time, the group of seven banded together to isolate, intimidate and bully. They did not hold back. At the time of the meeting the bullying had been going on for more than two weeks.

As this was the first time I was trying to combat bullying working in a group setting rather than with an individual, I wanted, even needed, it to work well. I went to great lengths to ensure everything was just right. I booked the school conference room and organised drinks and nibbles for the students so they would feel comfortable and not threatened. I was careful to avoid making the students feel accused or blamed. I was determined to seek their cooperation and assistance in solving a problem by appealing to empathy.

The meeting that followed became a point of great learning for me. I learnt not to be put off my main objective when things were discouraging. I share it with you in the hope that if, in your efforts, you encounter similar discouragement, and what you feel to be a disastrous meeting, you will hang in there and see things through to the end.

When I tried to commence this meeting and welcomed the group they immediately got sidetracked and ploughed into the drinks and nibbles. It was obvious the feast was a distraction, at least for this group. They made a number of comments thanking me for getting them out of class and expressing just how great this was: 'We should do this every Maths lesson.'

There was a very strong leader in this group and I knew who she was. The leader sat fairly quietly throughout but I was well aware that all the wisecracks and giggles the students made were made to impress her and get her approval. When I explained we were meeting together because Mary was upset, they began to laugh. It took some time to get them back on track, but I was determined to keep going. I tried again, this time reading Mary's impact statement. Her statement was moving and really very emotional. With every point there was more laughter. I could feel myself getting angry and I wanted to shift into teacher mode. I wanted to put a stop to this and tell them what I thought of their rudeness. I wanted to call the meeting off and send them back to class. I took some deep breaths and worked hard not to reveal my true feelings of anger and frustration.

The group became very vocal and started competing with each other to be heard. They were now determined to justify their treatment of Mary and explain why she deserved everything she was getting. As well as attempting to appeal to their sense of empathy, I was also being very careful not to use words that may imply any sort of accusation or blame. I was fighting the temptation to point out to them that what they were doing was actually bullying. I was fighting the urge to teach them about bullying and how dangerous it can be. At that time I believed that if I mentioned the word 'bullying' it would imply blame, get them offside and hinder my attempts to get them to cooperate. In later meetings, I discovered that teaching about bullying and its potential dangers was not only helpful, it was important and valuable in the process. Talking about bullying and sharing extra impact stories have been very powerful in establishing empathy and cooperation. I have also discovered that this can be introduced into the meeting in a manner that does not imply direct accusation or blame. However, in this first group meeting I was determined to avoid everything that I thought might be detrimental to the process, so I resisted the temptation to talk and teach about bullying. All I had to work with was the victim's impact statement which they didn't appear to be taking seriously.

As mentioned earlier, the story itself is of little importance in this method of overcoming bullying. However, these students taught me that even though knowing the story may not be important in achieving the desired outcome, the telling of their story definitely was. It was important for them to have the opportunity to tell their story and it was important that they felt heard. These students wanted to tell their story, and I wanted to steer them towards a solution. They wanted to be heard and I wanted to hear what they were prepared to do to help. They wanted to be listened to and understood, and I wanted a commitment and a solution.

They kept justifying and I kept steering. We were all getting frustrated. By this time all the drinks and nibbles had been demolished and the students had begun to make shapes and objects out of the polystyrene cups.

It seemed we were getting nowhere fast. Somehow I managed to hang in there and get things back on track, at least for a few moments. I reminded them that we had a problem and I was seeking their support to solve it. Then I asked them who was prepared to help. Six of the seven quickly raised their hands indicating they were, leaving the leader the only one with her hand down. Something interesting had happened here. The group dynamics and power had suddenly shifted and the numbers were against the leader. Prior to this, knowing who the leader was, I had been directing my attention and questions away from her, hoping the others would stand out on their own and change the group dynamics. Up to this point it wasn't working. The six left their hands in the air and looked at the leader. The leader slowly and hesitantly raised her hand to half-mast. Finally I had reached a point of consensus. There was now a group commitment to assist; now it was a matter of what they were prepared to do to help.

I decided to get each student in turn to state one thing they might do to help. Changing tack, I started with the leader. She was hesitant, but the others waited in anticipation. She finally decided that she would try to be nice to Mary. As we went around the group, a number of the students again became sidetracked and returned to aspects of the story that were important to them. I was learning that if I expected these students to cooperate and be helpful, I would need to listen and value their story. Their story was very different to Mary's story but I knew that finding or uncovering the truth was not the objective.

By the end of this, my first group meeting, I was ready to give up. I had had enough of their justification, light-hearted, non-serious, 'this is a joke' type responses and attitudes. Their inability to empathise and their reluctance to cooperate were frustrating. I was glad the meeting was over and more than happy to send them back to class.

This meeting made me feel low, disappointed, a failure, and in need of serious debriefing. I couldn't help but feel that the meeting was a total waste of time and effort. This first group meeting was indeed hard work and things hadn't proceeded the way I had expected or hoped. So much for the group idea, the drinks, the nibbles and the friendly, relaxed non-threatening setting. I'd be better off sticking to the individual sessions.

I was left pondering the possibility that I may have even made the situation worse for Mary. Later that evening as I was thinking through the session for the one millionth time, I realised that maybe it wasn't all that bad. Surely it was better that they were being honest and up front with me, than saying all the expected things and being dishonest. They had agreed to help, even though reluctantly. Why not just wait and see what happens and how things turn out.

The next morning I was greeted by their Maths teacher who enquired what had happened in the meeting the day before. I replied with a hesitant, concerned, 'Why? What has happened now?' He explained that the group returned to class all apologetic and were all over Mary like a rash. He explained that they had made every effort to be nice, but didn't overdo it. The students went out of their way to include Mary and the teacher believed they were being sincere. Personally, I was still doubtful and concerned that their reactions may not have been genuine or indeed sincere.

I called for Mary to see how she was coping and feeling about things. Mary was very happy and said she had been accepted back into the group. I didn't want her to know or pick up on my suspicions of insincerity, so I was careful with what I said. I must have followed up on this incident five or six times over the next few weeks. The desired result had been established. The victim was safe and felt safe, and the bullying behaviour had ceased, at least against Mary.

A week later a small section of the same group had been implicated in bullying a different student. Again I was disappointed and a little angry. Then I realised that:

- these students had had no teaching about what constitutes bullying, or the dangerous impact it can have on an individual.
- there had been no explanation of the school's policy, procedures and discipline plan when dealing with ongoing bullying issues.
- there were no deterrents or any system that made them accountable.

They simply stopped bullying one student and kept bullying another.

I went through the process again but this time the identified group was smaller. This time I taught them about bullying and why it can be so damaging. I outlined the school bullying policy, plan and the consequences that are in place for repeat offenders. I explained that because I had failed to inform them of these things, I believed it would be unfair to refer them to the coordinators for consequences. I made it clear that it would be recorded on file as a second offence. Any further incidents would be considered a third offence and viewed as extremely serious. They were left in no doubt that the coordinators and their parents would become involved if there were any future incidents of this kind.

The students were not accused and did not respond negatively. They were much more serious in attitude and even more willing to cooperate in finding a solution. They had an opportunity to tell their story and were listened to and supported. They were not judged or condemned, but were asked to share in the responsibility of finding a solution as well as take responsibility for their actions. All this happened without the distractions of drinks, nibbles and polystyrene cups. The bullying immediately stopped and follow-ups with the recipient over the next few weeks confirmed that this was so. An added advantage to using this method is that it has the potential to build positive relationships with students when previously you may not have had the opportunity. A number of the students involved in this incident have returned to me seeking personal support for non-related issues.

The first and subsequent group meeting taught me some important lessons and contributed much to the development of *shared responsibility*. We are emotional beings. *Shared responsibility* appeals to emotion. When as facilitators we experience negative emotions, it is important we do not fall victim to them. If I had reacted to my personal feelings and emotions and given up, I would have failed to learn a number of valuable lessons that further developed the method. Since that first group meeting, I have experienced many emotions but have disciplined myself to manage them, and not diverted from the method. The results have confirmed the power and effectiveness of the *shared responsibility* method.

CHAPTER EIGHT

KEEPING RECORDS

The fear of consequences is often more powerful than the implementation of consequences.

It is important for schools to have a central filing system that holds the records of all incidents of bullying that are processed through the *shared responsibility* meeting.

The *shared responsibility* meeting files are important and needed for:
- following up incidents,
- dealing with enquiries from parents or teachers,
- providing evidence in department or school investigations,
- identifying repeat offenders,
- identifying patterns of bullying that a particular student may be exhibiting,
- providing evidence and a basis for counselling referrals or school disciplinary action,
- providing evidence of school action and outcome.

All harassment incidents that are processed through the *shared responsibility* meeting should be recorded on a standard form. The Shared Responsibility Meeting Form (see Appendix One) includes:
- the name of the student accused of bullying,
- the name of the student with the concern,
- the date of the meeting,
- a number on the top of the form indicating whether the incident is the first, second, etc,
- the names of all the students who made up the group involved in the bullying,
- the source of referral, e.g. staff, parent, self, survey,
- the victim's impact statement,
- a space to indicate whether the student has been cooperative or uncooperative,
- the action the student decides to take to help solve the problem,

- a follow-up section,
- a space for teacher comments,
- incident details as reported by the recipient. This information will not be used in the *shared responsibility* meeting, but may be important if the school has to justify why a student's name has been placed on the harassment file, or if asked what the student was actually doing.

It is important that an individual form be filled out and filed for each student who has engaged in the bullying.

It is quick and easy to fill out a master form. All the basic information can be recorded on this form before the *shared responsibility* meeting. Prepare the master form this way.

- Leave the space for the name of the interviewed student blank.
- Record the date.
- Fill in all the names of the group members.
- Include the victim impact statement.
- Complete the incident details.

You can continue to make use of the master form during or immediately after the meeting. The personal response section and the section that indicates if the student has been cooperative or not can be filled in on the master form. If all the students are being cooperative and are willing to help, then just tick the 'cooperative' section. Most times the students will decide together what they will do to help. It is quick and easy to record all their responses on the one form. If an individual student has a different way of helping, record it using that student's name, e.g. Ben indicated that he would apologise.

After the meeting:

- Photocopy the master form according to the number of students in the group.
- Fill in the name of the individual student at the top of each form.
- Make any adjustments or comments that may apply to an individual student.
- Place the form in a manila folder marked with the student's name and file in the 'follow-up' section of the *shared responsibility* harassment file. The follow-up section is explained below.

Some schools like their coordinators to have a copy of each form for their personal records. If this is the case, photocopy each completed form and mark them 'File Only'. Doing this indicates to the coordinators that they do not need to follow up or take action on the report.

There may be some students who participate in the *shared responsibility* meeting who have not participated in the bullying activities. For example, Sarah may be part of the peer group and is always with them, but according to the recipient, never gets involved in the bullying. There is no need to fill in a form for Sarah but it is important to record her name as being a part of the group. Filling in or not filling in a form for Sarah is at the facilitator's discretion and should be based on the information provided by the bullied student. You may be tempted to leave Sarah out of the process altogether, but it is advisable she takes part. Bullying often works on group dynamics and Sarah is an important part of the group. She may contribute valuably in influencing the others and bring about positive change in attitude and behaviour. The only time you may consider leaving Sarah out of the process is when the group is too large. If Sarah were included in the meeting, there would be no need to fill in and file a form in her name, as she had not been a bully herself. This may need to be explained to her privately.

Students, by law, need to be informed that a record of the meeting is being kept on file. Inform them that this record includes the concern and what they are prepared to do to help solve the problem. It is advisable to read to the students what you have recorded on the form. It is important that:

- the students know and understand that the incident is being recorded on a standard form.
- the students know *what* you have recorded on the form. This includes the concern, the victim impact statement, what the students have decided to do to assist in solving the problem and the follow-up details that are all components of the Shared Responsibility Meeting Form.
- the students feel comfortable with the contents of the form.
- the students understand that a file exists in their name and they have a right to know what it contains.
- the students know that the information on the form will be referred to and used if there are future incidents.

After explaining and reading the contents of the form to the students make any necessary alterations if they feel the recorded information is inaccurate. This aspect of the method has the added impact and benefit of acting as a deterrent to the bullies. The bullies know and understand that the incident has been recorded in detail and it will not be put down somewhere and forgotten. The recording and filing of the incident makes it more difficult for a student to continue to bully without fear of detection or having to face the consequences of their actions. Most students will make an effort to avoid consequences if they can. The fear of consequences is often more powerful than the implementation of consequences, particularly when presented in an educational manner rather than a bullying or threatening one.

The Shared Responsibility Meeting Forms should be stored in a lockable filing cabinet. This filing system should accommodate three sections:

- The follow-up section. This section is for storing files of the cases still alive. When the *shared responsibility* meeting is completed, the forms should be filed here. It is best to file them in order of incident. This makes it easier to know which cases need to be followed up first. New cases should be filed at the back. These files will work their way forward as other cases are completed and transferred to the general file section. On average a file will be in the follow-up section for about three weeks.
- The general section. This section is for storing all files of the finalised cases. After adequate follow-up and monitoring, the files are transferred to this section. The files can be organised in alphabetical order, or in year levels, home groups, or any way that meets the needs of the structure of the school.
- The stationery and data section. This section is for storing unused forms, surveys, survey data and other bullying related materials.

The filing cabinet should be kept locked and the key stored in a central place where it can be accessed easily by the appropriate staff. If schools use other forms for initial referrals, they should be attached to the Shared Responsibility Meeting Form and filed together.

When a student has been implicated as engaging in bullying, the first point of reference should be the *shared responsibility* file. This file will indicate if a student has engaged in bullying previously, and make it easy to identify what action, if any, has already been taken. A quick glance at the file will indicate what stage of the method needs now to be implemented. If a student's name is not on file it should mean they have not been implicated in bullying before. Make sure you look in both sections of the file and check with other staff who may have removed the file for some reason, or be working with the student on another bullying case.

The filing system is user friendly and practical. It makes it easy for a school to keep bullying issues separated from general behavioural issues. It is also helpful in identifying, picking up, and following up those students who may be exhibiting problems in complying with acceptable, safe behavioural practices and expectations.

CHAPTER NINE

DEALING WITH REPEAT OFFENDERS—THE SECOND MEETING

A part of our learning is to realise that in the real world there are consequences for our actions.

When facing a second *shared responsibility* meeting, approach it in the same way as you did the first meeting. The objectives remain the same—to help the victim be safe and feel safe, as well as to put a stop to the bullying. In a second meeting you again approach the issue in a non-threatening, non-blaming manner. You will again be seeking the assistance of the student to help solve a problem.

The second *shared responsibility* meeting may differ from the first meeting in the following ways:

- you may choose to work with individual students rather than with groups of students,
- there will be more emphasis on welfare support for the bully and exploration of what may be going on for them that is causing them to bully,
- when concluding, you will consider the need to share the responsibility more widely and make a referral to the school disciplinary staff, so they then become involved in the process.

Working with individual students rather than with groups is suggested because the 'accused' student may be the only second time offender in a particular group. The first and second meeting procedures are slightly different, so having a mixture of both first and second time offenders will make the process difficult for the facilitator to manage effectively. Also, issues that require confidentiality can arise when exploring the reasons behind 'why' a student has continued to bully.

Begin the second meeting in a similar way to the first. Welcome the students and thank them for coming. In the second meeting include an extra thank you for the way the student assisted in solving the previous problem. Explain that as far as you are aware, everything turned out well. Explain that you have called them in to seek their help in solving another problem. You may go about it this way, assuming that the second offence has been directed at a different target:

> Come in Michael. Thanks for coming. Take a seat. You helped me solve a problem a while back and I am hoping you will be able to help me again. By the way, thanks for what you did. As far as I know everything turned out well, so you must have done a good job. Recently I have been speaking with Chris and I found out that he is not a happy person at the moment. Do you have any idea what is going on?

At the appropriate time in the meeting include the recipient's impact statement and remind the student of the serious consequences that bullying can have on a person. There is no need to go into the big teaching spiel as you did at the first meeting.

If a student is continuing to bully there will be reasons behind their behaviour. Explore, with the student, what is happening for them and how they feel about school, friends, home and peers. Sometimes bullying is the result, or symptomatic, of other personal problems. It is not unusual for a bullied student to find a weaker student to bully in an effort to restore some sense of lost power or self-esteem. Be sensitive with your enquiries, particularly about home. Some students are open to talking about school but feel threatened or uncomfortable talking about home issues. Some students may consider this to be intrusive and unsafe to talk about. You can approach the home issue sensitively by asking, 'Have you told anyone at home about what is happening for you at school, your mum or dad?'

It is important that you listen, care for and support the student. If the student is being bullied, explain that there are ways in which you can help them learn to deal with the problem. If the student is fearful or reluctant to involve teachers, offer some support that may be helpful, without involving the teachers. This will nearly always involve the student trusting someone enough to talk about it. Ask, 'If I can arrange it, would you like to speak to someone about what's happening?' Make a referral if necessary, or personally introduce them to someone who will support them if you are unable to do it yourself. If they are reluctant ask, 'How are you dealing with the issue at the moment? Is it working for you?'

Do not lose sight of the purpose of this meeting. If contributing factors are uncovered, the student should be referred to support staff or, if you decide to deal with the issues yourself, schedule an appointment for another time.

As a part of the second *shared responsibility* meeting, seek a commitment from the student to help solve the bullying problem you are presently facing. Write down what the student is prepared to do to help. Follow the same record-keeping procedure as used in the first meeting, only this time record it as a second incident. Explain to the student that because this is a second incident, you are required to make a referral to the school's disciplinary staff. Inform the student that there may be consequences this time. It is useful to prepare the student for this meeting as well as remind them of the school's policy and procedures if there are future incidents.

You may say it like this:

> Michael, you helped us last time to solve a problem and it's great that you are willing to help again. If you do what you say you will; the problem will be fixed. You need to understand that because this is a second incident, the school requires me to refer this matter to the disciplinary staff. When you speak with them, inform them that you have spoken with me and what you have decided to do to fix the problem. Explain that you have learnt from what has happened and that you will not do it again. Michael, the school is not out to hurt, or get you, we want to help. A part of our learning is to realise that in the real world there are consequences for our actions. You have cooperated in the past and I see no reason why you won't do it again. Do you think you can fix it? (Get a commitment.) Explain to the disciplinary staff that the problem is already fixed and they may take this into account when considering your consequences. This will be recorded and filed as a second incident. Any future incidents will be considered very seriously and the disciplinary staff will be involved again. There will be further consequences and your parents will be invited in to discuss the matter with us. The school can't stand back and allow such incidents to continue, do you understand this Michael? We might have to look more deeply into why you feel the need to hurt others.

The discipline or consequence component of the *shared responsibility* method is important and effective in working with repeat offenders of bullying. Some other methods devised for overcoming bullying in schools have disregarded the administration of discipline and consequences altogether. Appealing only to empathy does not take into account that people can, and do, learn by consequences.

We learn not to break the law because we might end up in prison or financially penalised. We learn that if we treat people badly it will impact on our relationships and sense of belonging. We learn that if we break a rule, there are appropriate consequences.

Shared responsibility puts welfare, education and the appeal to empathy before the administration of consequences, but this does not lessen the importance and impact of explained consequences in beating bullying.

I have learnt that:

- dealing with bullying solely as a behavioural issue and endeavouring to beat it with punishment alone is rarely effective.
- trying to change the behaviours of bullies by bullying or threatening the bullies is also ineffective.
- relying solely on the appeal to empathy is limited and leaves a school with nowhere to go if a student doesn't respond or bullies again.
- relying solely on education and awareness programs does not have a lasting or ongoing impact.
- treating students with respect, getting them onside, caring for and listening to them, empowering them to act and share the responsibility in solving a problem, teaching them about bullying and the possible impact of their behaviour, as well as teaching them about the possible consequences of their behaviour, is very powerful and effective in beating bullying.

The inclusion of consequences in the *shared responsibility* method is intended to:

- help the bullying student learn and take responsibility for their actions.
- teach the bullying student about life and that there are consequences, both natural and applied, to a person's choices.
- act as a deterrent to those students who are inclined to bully. Most students will cooperate and avoid consequences if they can.
- make a statement to the bullying student and the school community that ongoing bullying is serious and will not be allowed to continue.
- help the bullied student and others affected by it feel supported, and let them know that justice is being done and the bullies are being held accountable.

The welfare and educational components of the method should be kept separate from the discipline procedures. Consequences should be administered by a person other than the *shared responsibility* meeting facilitator. The facilitator of the meeting should:

- make it clear to the student that their role is to help them find a solution to the problem.
- support the student by assisting them to work through the issues to ensure that it won't happen again.

- inform the student that they are required by the school to refer the matter to the discipline staff.
- make it clear to the student that the discipline process is out of their (the facilitator's) hands and control.
- organise any referrals that may be required.
- ensure the students are followed up and the paperwork completed.

Consequences should be incident related. Students need to see a connection between what they have done and the consequences they are receiving. If they have caused others to feel unsafe in the yard, the bullying student should have restricted yard usage for a time, or different break times. Detentions can be useful if the bullying student understands the reason why they are not allowed in the yard for a period of time. It is up to the school to decide on the appropriate consequences. It is important that the consequences not only be explained to the student, but they be administered in a calm and respectful manner without anger. The staff needs to model appropriate behaviour that cannot be interpreted by the students as resembling bullying. This is a sensitive issue in schools but it can't be let pass without comment. Unfortunately, some teachers survive using aggressive bullying tactics. There should not be one expectation for students and another for staff. Staff need to model the behaviour they expect from their students. If staff are going to yell and scream at students then they shouldn't be surprised when a student yells back. This does not mean a teacher cannot use a little volume and tone when responding to breaches of discipline, but it does mean they need to display self-control and respect.

It is advisable that the second *shared responsibility* meeting take place before the disciplinary staff become involved, but this may not always be possible or practical. If the disciplinary staff understand and support the *shared responsibility* method, they will refer the matter to the *shared responsibility* meeting facilitator first. If this doesn't happen, then adapt the procedure to a post-disciplinary one.

You could commence the meeting this way:

> I know the disciplinary staff have already spoken to you about this matter. It's not my place to interfere with that and I won't. I would like to discuss with you how we can work together to fix the situation and make sure that this doesn't continue or happen again. If we can do this, we can avoid any further trouble. I am seeking your help in solving this problem in the same way as you helped last time.

Complete the second *shared responsibility* meeting in the same way as you did the first meeting. Thank the student for their help and wish them well. Offer any further support if you feel they need it. Remind the student that you will follow up with them and the victim to see how things are going. On the rare occasion when the student refuses to cooperate, refer the matter directly to the disciplinary staff. This has only occurred once in my many *shared responsibility* meetings, and this student changed his attitude after listening to a number of impact statements that obviously moved him.

We are not out to punish or seek revenge; we are out to ensure the victim is safe, feels safe and the bullying ceases.

Now that I have outlined the process involved in the second *shared responsibility* meeting, I'm going to run the risk of confusing you a little by outlining a possible variation to the process. In the first *shared responsibility* meeting (see Chapter 6), it was pointed out to the bully/ies that a second offence *may* involve consequences, not necessarily *will*.

There are many possible contributing factors to consider when deciding what is the best way to respond to and deal with second-time offenders of bullying.

Factors to consider include:
- the length of time between offences—there may be a time gap of a year or more,
- outside provocation or involvement that has kept the issue alive,
- long-lasting competitive type disputes between the students involved,
- old conflict issues that have never been resolved,
- it may be a conflict, not bullying, issue.

Do not accept family problems or anger management issues as an excuse for ongoing bullying. A student should be supported in dealing with these concerns but it is never a justification for bullying.

However, we must take into account that the *shared responsibility* meeting is an educational exercise and allowances may need to be made for those students who do not grasp things easily, or learn as quickly as others.

The objectives of *shared responsibility* are to ensure the victim is safe, feels safe and to put a stop to bullying. If these objectives can be reached fairly, without the need for consequences, it is at the facilitator's discretion if a referral needs to be made to the disciplinary staff. Imagine that 18 months ago a Year 7 student went through his first *shared responsibility* meeting. The student was responsive and helpful. Everything worked well. The bullying stopped and the desired outcome was achieved. There have not been any further reports of bullying by this student since that time. This boy is now in Year 9 and a new bullying concern has arisen with a different victim. Is it fair to this student or helpful to the process if he is automatically referred to the disciplinary staff for consequences? At least the student deserves the right to talk, explain the issue and fix things up if he can. It is easy to jump to conclusions and revert to 'teacher mode' if a report is made about a known offender. It is important to stay calm and not jump to any preconceived conclusions.

In the early days of developing and testing the *shared responsibility* method, I was informed that a student had engaged in bullying for a second time. At first I was angry, annoyed, and disappointed that I may be faced with the method's first failure. I quickly settled down, content and eager to test stage two of the new method. During what was meant to be the second *shared responsibility* meeting, the bullying student, who was being friendly, polite and cooperative, indicated sincerely that he didn't know what I was talking about.

Further investigation indicated that a new student to the school was trying to establish position and a social connection within his new peer group. He somehow became aware of the past problem and tried to become popular by stirring it up. It was a way for him to climb the social ladder of acceptance. He moved between two social groups stirring, making things up, and passing messages back and forth. Threats were being made up and passed on by him, and exaggerated responses were bouncing back.

Fortunately, the original target fulfilled his responsibilities and immediately reported what he thought was a renewed attack of bullying. In following the matter up further, the recipient confirmed that the threats had not come to him directly, but had in fact been delivered by this new student. The recipient had wrongly thought the new student was his friend. Such threats had in fact not been made. Fortunately the potential conflict between the two groups was avoided and there was no need for a bullying interview, at least not with the accused student.

If the matter is straightforward and the second time offender is bullying, a referral should be made and the process followed. On the other hand, if there are other contributing factors to consider such as those I have listed above and the student is being cooperative, helpful, and the objectives are more easily and fairly obtained without a referral, then don't make one.

A 'discipline referral' is often a good carrot to dangle in a second meeting with a student. You may explain at some point during the meeting that the school requires you to make a referral to the disciplinary staff, but you are uncertain if it is the best thing to do in their case. Enquire if the student feels that the problem can be better solved without getting the 'heavies' involved. If this is the case, seek a commitment from the student of the ways in which they can help.

If you decide that a referral is not needed, explain to the student why you have decided this. It is still important that this be recorded as a second incident.

You could explain it like this:

Michael, you helped us last time to solve a problem and I believe that you can help to fix this one. If you cooperate and do what you say you will, then the matter will be fixed. If it is fixed, then I see no need to refer this to the disciplinary staff. The reasons I'm doing this are because it has been over a year since the last incident and I don't really see you as a bully. You have cooperated in the past and I see no reason why you won't do it again. Do you think you can fix things up without the need for going to the disciplinary staff? (*Seek a commitment.*) I do have to record this and it will be on file as a second incident. Michael, you need to understand that if there is any future incident the disciplinary staff will definitely be involved and your parents will be invited in to discuss the matter with us. The school can't stand back and allow bullying to continue, do you understand?

Conclude the meeting in the same way as the first meeting by thanking them for their assistance and remind them that you will be following up with them and the victim.

When a bullying incident involves both first and second time offenders, the *shared responsibility* meeting can be run as a first meeting. The second time offenders will benefit from the revision process. Once the group has made a commitment to help and the action decided on, the first time offender/s should be thanked and dismissed. Keep the second time offender/s back to complete the process as outlined above. If during the meeting you discover that what is occurring is not bullying and you decide that the issue is better referred to mediation or another support process, the Shared Responsibility Meeting Form need not be filled in and filed.

Repeat offenders are uncommon using the *shared responsibility* method. However, no matter how effective a method is in overcoming bullying, we must allow for the possibility that some students will re-offend and schools need to be prepared for and respond to this. In the first meeting the responsibility is shared between the victim, the perpetrator and the facilitator. In the second meeting, personal issues of the perpetrator are explored and the responsibility may be shared more widely by involving the disciplinary staff of the school. In the case where a third meeting is required, the responsibility is further expanded to engage the assistance and support of the parents.

CHAPTER TEN

DEALING WITH REPEAT OFFENDERS—THE THIRD MEETING

At this point it is necessary to share the responsibility with the parents.

The third *shared responsibility* meeting takes on a different format from the first two meetings. By now the bullying student will have gone through the processes of welfare support, education, counselling and consequences. When a student continues to bully beyond this, it reveals a deeper problem that will probably require more professional evaluation, assistance and support. At this point it is necessary to share the responsibility with the parents.

The school needs to be clear and certain that the bullying is continuing to occur. Blake was accused of bullying another student a week before his Year 7 camp. He had been through the first *shared responsibility* meeting and responded well, and was cooperative and willing to help. I followed up with his victim on a daily basis before and during the camp. Everything was reported to be fine— even better than fine. On the day before the camp a parent reported that Blake was bullying their son and they were concerned about it happening on camp. The morning of the camp another parent raised a similar concern about Blake, requesting the staff keep a close eye on him during the camp. Both these reports were passed on to the teacher in charge of the camp and I was informed that disciplinary sanctions may need to be put in place. Because of time restraints I was unable to catch up with the recipients before the camp. Bullying is all about the victim so it was important for me to speak with these students before following up with Blake. As the last two bullying reports were made only days after my meeting with Blake, I was hesitant to act hastily, unsure if Blake was continuing to bully, or that the parents were reporting incidents that had occurred prior to the *shared responsibility* meeting.

I urged the staff to be patient and tread carefully. In following up at the camp with the recipients, everything pointed to incidents that had occurred before Blake's meeting. These students had expressed to their parents their discomfort in being on a camp with Blake. Their discomfort was based on a number of incidents that had occurred a week or more earlier. The parents naturally believed that the bullying was still a problem and were concerned about the safety of their children while they were away. To Blake's credit, all reports indicated that he had not bullied since the meeting. It appears that prior to our meeting, Blake had been quite busy throwing his weight around in an effort to make a name for himself. In doing so, he had managed to upset a number of students. It would have been unfair and detrimental to Blake to treat him as a second and third time offender based on these reports.

After a student has continued with his or her bullying, he or she should be called in and informed that another incident has been reported. The student should have the opportunity to explain and cooperate in solving the problem. The student is to be informed that a meeting is to be arranged with their parents. The parents will be invited to share the responsibility and assist in finding a solution to what is now emerging as a serious problem.

You may approach the topic this way:

> Michael, I have called you in to inform you that you have been implicated in another bullying incident. It is important that we get your side of the story and find out what is happening. There are always two sides to every story. I was asked to talk with Sean about why he has not been coming to school. He informed me that he is feeling unsafe and hates it here. What's going on Michael?

> This is the third time I have been asked to talk to you about bullying. You understand what bullying is, and that it can have a serious impact on some students. You have told me that you believe bullying is bad and yet you keep landing in the middle of it. Last time the disciplinary staff were involved and I believe you were suspended for a few days. To your credit Michael, you have always been cooperative and willing to help find a solution. What we don't understand is why this is continuing to occur. Michael, you need to know that your parents will be invited in to meet with the disciplinary staff and myself. We will be asking them to share the responsibility in helping us find a solution to this ongoing concern. If you can fix the problem before they come it will be helpful. We need to assist you in learning how to contribute to this school in a more positive way. We will explore with your parents ways we may be able to help you. Because this is a third offence,

there will be further consequences and it may mean a longer suspension. It may be helpful for you to inform your parents that we will be in touch. It would be better if they hear it from you first.

The third *shared responsibility* meeting should be arranged and controlled by the school administration or disciplinary staff who will call upon the support of the welfare staff. The meeting should include the parents, a representative of the school administration, the staff member responsible for the discipline of students and, if available, the staff member who facilitated the first and second *shared responsibility* meetings. It is important that a member of the school welfare team attends this meeting. The student may be invited to the meeting depending on the wishes of the school and/or the parents. You may wish to discuss the issue initially with the parents without the student being present. The student can be called in at a later stage. It is important that the student be involved at some stage. They need to take responsibility for what is happening, and they need to be involved in, and own, the process. The parents are to be invited to share the responsibility in finding a solution to the ongoing concern.

The welfare staff will outline:

- the concern,
- the incidents that have occurred to date,
- the approach the school has taken in each case,
- the support given and offered to the student so far.

It should be explained to the parents, that because this behaviour has been ongoing and a pattern has emerged, there is the need for further intervention and support. It should be explained that their child, even though cooperative in solving individual problems, has not responded as well as you had hoped he or she would in ceasing with the bullying activities. To this point the welfare support, teaching, counselling and the school-administered consequences have been ineffective in overcoming the ongoing bullying problem.

The school support services should be outlined and an appropriate plan of action agreed to and followed. This may include a psychological evaluation and, if deemed necessary, ongoing counselling. The school may require a school youth worker, chaplain or other support person be involved at this stage. Referral to a support group that has been set up to assist students to learn responsible behaviour is yet another consideration. Providing parents with contact details of outside school agencies and support services would be practical as well as helpful.

The disciplinary staff should explain to the parents the school's responsibility to impose appropriate consequences, and what they will be. These may involve suspension. They should inform the parents of the school's responsibility to provide and maintain a safe, supportive environment for all students, including their child.

The aim of the third *shared responsibility* meeting is to involve the parents, and further strengthen the student's support team. Avoid conflict. Accusations, blame and threats are not helpful and achieve little. Parents will be naturally defensive of their children and are more likely to be supportive if they know you care for their child and have the child's best interest at heart.

The parents need to understand that if the pattern continues the school will administer further consequences and will be taking the matter very seriously. It is important that the parents understand the seriousness of the problem. It is even more important that they understand the school has the wellbeing and welfare of their child at heart, as well as every other student in the school.

Students who will not avail themselves of the support offered to them, who do not respond positively to counselling or psychological support, who will not work in cooperation with the school to ensure a safe environment for all students, may be asked to consider finding another school. The school will have solid evidence of policy, procedure, incidents, support rendered and offered, as well as the consequences administered over a period of time. Any further expectations placed on the school are unreasonable. It is not practical to expect a school to provide support or services beyond those which have been listed above. It is not reasonable for a school to tolerate a student who is a constant threat to the safety and wellbeing of other students. Bullying cannot be tolerated.

Another *shared responsibility* interview form should be completed and filed. It should record what the school, the parents and the students are prepared to do to solve the problem.

CHAPTER ELEVEN

SEARCHING FOR FACTS AND FINDING THE TRUTH

He stood alone as a victim, he now stood alone as one accused of lying, or as one in need of providing proof to substantiate his suffering and pain.

Schools have battled long and hard over the years to find better ways to respond to bullying effectively. In this chapter I want to challenge the myth that searching for facts, and finding the truth, is helpful in beating bullying. One of the most common methods used in schools is what I will call, for want of a better name 'The Detective Method'. This method includes:

- investigating the incident,
- interviewing witnesses,
- taking statements,
- gathering evidence,
- searching for and finding the truth,
- prosecuting and punishing.

Many schools persist with this approach even though it is ineffective, time consuming and potentially damaging to the victims. Investigations take time and they rarely produce the information needed to solve a bullying problem. The experience of those who work in schools is that:

- witnesses can prove unreliable. They often don't see anything, or they provide conflicting stories.
- statements are often conflicting or point blame back at the victim.
- friends lie to protect friends.
- accused students become defensive and uncooperative.
- evidence is difficult to uncover in support of the claims of an already unpopular, socially isolated victim.
- students are reluctant to speak up in fear of becoming a victim themselves or being seen as a dobber.

The truth is, in pursuing these things a school runs the risk of placing further stress and pressure on a possibly already traumatised victim. Even if it were possible to find the truth and gather enough evidence to prove that a student has been bullying, it does nothing to address or rectify the bullying problem.

A teacher suspected that Nigel was being bullied. She had noticed a group of boys in the class making fun of him and that Nigel was not responding or accepting this well. Nigel began to sit by himself and withdraw from his class. The concerned teacher kept Nigel back after class one day and enquired if he was OK. At first Nigel pretended things were fine, but then appeared hesitant and fearful when about to leave the room. The teacher noticed a group of boys waiting outside and asked if Nigel was worried about them. Nigel began to cry. The teacher recorded the names of the boys in the group and referred the matter to the year level coordinator. Nigel and the other boys were called out of class and the coordinator enquired if there was a problem. Nigel remained silent and the boys in the group insisted everything was fine. The bullying got worse and Nigel began to stay away from school.

A few weeks later the coordinator called home to enquire about Nigel's absences. His mother expressed concern about Nigel saying that he had been very sick and unwilling to come to school. She had taken him to the doctor who confirmed that there was nothing physically wrong with him. A meeting was scheduled to discuss the matter further. Nigel, his mum and the coordinator met at the school a few days later. Nigel reluctantly indicated that he felt unsafe in his class. The coordinator said that he would look into the matter but the most important thing was to get Nigel back in school. The meeting resulted in Nigel returning to school the next day.

At recess Nigel found himself trapped in the middle of a group of tormenting, aggressive boys who were trying to incite a fight between him and one of the boys in the group. A teacher on yard duty noticed what was happening and escorted the group, including Nigel to the coordinator's office. Nigel tried to be brave and tell the coordinator privately about what had happened. The coordinator got all the boys together and informed them that he was going to get to the bottom of this and put a stop to it. The boys were seated at different points in a corridor and instructed to write a statement about what had happened in the yard. Nigel knew that the numbers were stacked against him. He knew that all the others would stick together and that his story would be different from theirs. He felt that no one cared. No one was prepared to listen or believe him. In his mind, even his mum had abandoned him by making him attend school. He was on his own; there was no one on his side and there was nothing he could do about it.

The coordinator spent considerable time reading the statements, trying to ascertain what was going on and what had really happened. The most compelling evidence was that there was an overwhelming belief among the students that Nigel had started it and was to blame. The coordinator interviewed a few reliable and trusted members of the class to see if they could shed some light on the problem, but they couldn't, or wouldn't. One student confirmed that she saw Nigel in the yard with the group that recess, and it looked like he was in for a fight. The coordinator also spoke individually to each of the group members. By this time the group members were beginning to become defensive and angry, denying doing anything wrong and resentful for being blamed for something they insisted they didn't do. They stuck to their stories and insisted that Nigel had started it. They consistently appealed to their friends for support and to confirm their stories.

The coordinator spoke with Nigel again. With a strong and firm tone in his voice the coordinator confronted him with the group's account of events. He informed Nigel that from what he was able to find out after reading the statements and speaking to the other students involved, as well as other members of the class, it appeared that he had not been totally truthful in all this. Nigel tried to tell him about all the things that had been happening to him, but the coordinator interrupted, stating that Nigel could not just accuse people without providing the proof to support his claims. He stood alone as a victim, he now stood alone as one accused of lying, or as one in need of providing proof to substantiate his suffering and pain. Nigel was not helped by insensitive comments from the coordinator such as:

'Maybe you can try being a bit more friendly Nigel.'

'There are better ways of dealing with your frustrations other than fighting.'

'Lighten up a little, don't take everything so seriously.'

Deep down, I believe the coordinator knew that Nigel was the real victim, but from his investigations he was unable to prove it. It was easier for him to walk the safe and neutral road.

In the end the coordinator decided to issue a three day suspension to the two boys who were involved in the 'nearly fight'. Nigel was one of them. The other boys were spoken to firmly and warned that if they were involved in something like this again they too would be suspended. This was a verbal deterrent. Nothing was recorded other than the needed paper work relating to the suspensions.

After the suspension, Nigel was labelled by the whole class as a dobber. He was relentlessly tormented, accused and blamed for getting another fellow student, Brian, in trouble and suspended. He was never again accepted as a member of that class. The bullying was unrelenting and Nigel continued to suffer alone. His concerned teacher spoke to him occasionally offering him support, 'If you like Nigel, I will speak to the coordinator about what is going on, to see if we can help', but Nigel refused, pleading to the teacher not to say anything to anyone. A few months later Nigel's parents moved him to another school. The problem simply went away.

Let us consider for a moment the school's objectives and methods in responding to this problem. I believe the school acted sincerely and intended to:

- deal with the problem as effectively and efficiently as possible,
- solve the problem by instigating an investigation,
- take statements from all who were involved in an effort to understand the problem,
- seek the cooperation of all the students involved,
- find the story and uncover the truth,
- seek and interview witnesses in an attempt to substantiate statements,
- weigh up all the evidence and establish which students were at fault,
- impose punishment, discipline, consequences or make the guilty students accountable,
- bring the problem to a satisfactory conclusion.

These intentions are all good. It appears the school took the matter seriously and put time and effort into addressing the problem. It is the method that needs to come under scrutiny. Consider the outcomes connected with various aspects of the method.

- The overall investigation was time consuming and non-productive.
- The taking of statements confused and complicated the matter. It also placed the victim under further pressure with the need to substantiate his story. He even felt the coordinator was against him.
- Efforts to uncover and find the truth proved frustrating and unfruitful. The truth was never uncovered.
- The witnesses proved unhelpful and, in some cases, confused the matter.
- The bullying students became defensive and uncooperative.
- The bullying students were not held accountable and nothing was accomplished that suggests they had learnt a lesson and would not bully again.
- The problem was not resolved and the bullying continued unchallenged.
- The process left the victim in a more helpless and vulnerable state than he was in the beginning. The victim suffered, and then suffered more.
- The victim became the accused and was punished.
- The victim left the school.

If the school was asked at the beginning of this process what outcomes they were hoping to achieve, I'm sure they would not have included any of the above.

Nigel's story is not an uncommon one. Even if Nigel had done or said something in the beginning that initiated the problem, and there is no indication that he did, this is not an excuse or justification for bullying. His torment was severe and ongoing. The numbers and the power were definitely against him. Bullying is about power, it is the abuse of power, and the school should have been able to recognise this and respond to it more appropriately.

The school tried to respond to bullying as they would with other problems such as a conflict, behavioural or peer group issue. Bullying is different and requires a different approach. In reality this school failed:
- to identify and respond to bullying in an effective manner,
- to provide a safe environment for the student,
- in their duty of care toward all the students.

This sounds serious and rather harsh but bullying is a serious issue. Nigel was not only a victim of his tormentors; he was a victim of his own school's procedures.

The Detective Method in responding to bullying can:
- place a teacher or staff member in a the stressful position of having to play policeman, prosecutor, lawyer, judge and jury, all at the same time,
- result in the accused feeling angry, aggrieved and unfairly treated,
- result in the accused going after their victims with even more vengeance than they did before,
- cause the bullying to be pushed underground and make it more difficult to detect and monitor,
- leave the victim in a worse position than before,
- create an environment where bullying can prosper and grow.

When dealing with bullying issues, it doesn't matter if you:
- discover the stories are different,
- suspect a student is not telling the truth,
- are unclear about what really happened.

Save yourself time and effort by forgetting about the witnesses, the statements and the many unnecessary interviews. Accept and listen to all stories without judgement. What has happened is not as important as what is going to happen. Remain neutral and solution focused, not fact focused. Focus all your attention on empowering the students to assist in finding a solution and supporting the victim.

Finding the truth and getting the story isn't important in beating bullying. The truth that really needs to be acknowledged is that you may have students in your school suffering in isolation and in serious need of help. The most important person in responding to bullying is the victim. The victim is to be supported and the bullying should be stopped. Schools need to seriously consider the methods they are using to combat bullying and constantly measure the effectiveness of these methods. Fact-finding is about blame and punishment. *Shared responsibility* is about working together to establish and maintain a safe supportive environment for all students.

CHAPTER TWELVE

DEALING WITH 'CHALLENGING' STUDENTS

My feelings of doubt and nervousness were magnified when confronted with the 'challenging' student.

By 'challenging', I refer to those students who are known for their unacceptable behaviour and attitude; students who have a reputation for being defensive, argumentative, aggressive and less than cooperative with the teaching staff.

For a period of time, I experienced a degree of discomfort and nervousness when faced with the task of confronting students accused of bullying. No matter how successful the *shared responsibility* method had been, I have always had to fight a little battle within myself. It was a battle with doubt: will this be effective with every student? It was also fighting the fear of the possibility of my first *shared responsibility* failure. Of course, I know the method really can't fail, it only proceeds to the next stage. My feelings of doubt and nervousness were magnified when confronted with the challenging student. I have always been motivated by a challenge so I was determined to give it a go. However, I do confess to struggling with the temptation to do things differently. The *shared responsibility* method needed to be tried and tested, and the challenging student provided the ideal opportunity to unleash and prove the method's real potential.

When facing the challenging student, simply stick with the method. Don't change a thing. I have been surprised and emotionally moved many times by the empathy, understanding, responses and cooperation of these students. In many cases I have found them to be more understanding, responsive and eager to help than those students who I may have considered to be less challenging.

I didn't realise how she was feeling and I felt bad

Glenda was a Year 8 student who had caused the school and all her teachers considerable concern from the day she arrived. She spent much of her time in 'timeout' or outside the Assistant Principal's office. When she was named as one of a group of three girls who were bullying another student my first thought was 'Oh no, this method won't work with Glenda.' Motivated by the challenge and wanting some hard cases to test my theories and method, I nervously decided to give it a go. None of these girls were known bullies as such, but they were tough and did not tolerate nonsense from anyone, including staff.

Karen, the girl they were bullying had been pushed up against walls, tripped, threatened, called names, laughed at, humiliated and attacked in a number of hostile and aggressive ways. This had been happening on a daily basis over a period of about two weeks. During this time, Karen had been trying hard to avoid these girls, school and going to the toilets. She was hiding in what she thought were the safest areas in the schoolyard. At the end of the school day Karen would run for her bus for fear of being bashed and caught on her own. When I was introduced to Karen she was extremely nervous. She was jumping and flinching at sudden movements as well as at any student group who came near or approached her. In her mind it appeared that her tormentors were hiding somewhere in the middle of every crowd.

In seeking the assistance of Glenda and her friends, I was surprised that they didn't even know the name of the girl they were bullying. When I explained the way their victim was feeling, the girls outlined what Karen had said and done to them that started it all. These girls didn't take rubbish from anyone and they bragged that Karen wasn't big enough to back up her mouth with actions. I listened to them and explained that I could understand why they would be upset and feeling the way they were.

I followed this up with a question type statement. 'So you decided to solve the problem by bullying her?' Glenda responded by saying, 'I didn't think of it like that, we just did it.'

A discussion followed as to whether the girls thought bullying was good or bad. They all insisted it was bad. 'Why is it bad? What is bullying?' I like to use the word 'bullying' as it has an unacceptable connotation to it. Many teachers avoid using the word, but I encourage it. If you ask a student, 'Are you bullying?' that student immediately associates the word 'bullying' with unacceptable or negative social behaviour. They know it is wrong.

As the discussion continued I took the opportunity to share Karen's impact statement and some of the stories that had caused me to take bullying very seriously. Glenda and one of the other girls were obviously moved. When I asked what they could do to help they started talking over each other in an attempt to get in first. I had to slow them down and caution them about approaching Karen as a group. Glenda and another girl wanted to apologise and explain to Karen why they were upset and that it was over now and they would not bother her again. They wanted it to happen immediately. The other student decided it was best just to back off and not go after her any more.

It was recess when we finished the meeting and I was concerned these girls might over-enthusiastically approach Karen and cause her to panic. Glenda and her friend approached Karen as cautiously as they could, but unfortunately Karen started to panic when some of her peers shouted out to her, 'Watch out Karen, they're coming.'

Glenda and her friend apologised and instantly alleviated Karen's fear. They explained why they had done what they did and that it was over now. They promised her that they would not bother her again and went to considerable lengths to make her feel safe. The other girl just kept her distance as she said she would. I followed up immediately to make sure Karen was OK. Karen was surprised and a little overwhelmed by what had happened. She felt happy and safe for the first time in two weeks. I followed up again and again over the next week. After three weeks it was, to the girls, a fading memory of some incident in their distant past.

After about four weeks had passed I noticed that Glenda was again sitting outside the Assistant Principal's office. I explained to her that I was writing a book and it would be valuable for me to know what made her change and stop bullying? Without hesitation she said, 'I didn't realise how she was feeling and I felt bad.'

This might be more difficult than I first expected

Alex was a fourteen year old, Year 9 student. Alex's bullying problem started on a Year 9 and 10 surfing camp. A group of three Year 10 boys chose Alex as an object for their amusement and fun. It originally started as a joke with just a bit of mimicking, but the boys soon started competing against each other to see who could be the funniest and most effective. Like many boys, Alex felt the need to deal with the situation himself, so he told no one. He tried a number of ways of coping and getting them to stop. Laughing with them didn't work for Alex as he was never going to be accepted by their group. He simply was not their type. Ignoring them in the hope they would tire of their little game had no impact either. Alex didn't realise that the purpose of their game wasn't so much to hurt him as it was to impress and upstage other members of the group. Alex's reactions were simply the measuring gauge to score their level of success.

Alex hoped that things would improve with the conclusion of the camp and their return to school. Alex didn't share any classes with these boys so he thought he would be able to avoid them and the problem would simply disappear. The boys hung out near the school canteen, an area that Alex found impossible to avoid all the time. Every time the boys saw him, their efforts and Alex's humiliation escalated. They were having a lot of fun at his expense. Alex's frustration level had grown to the point of anger. One day he became so angry that he approached the group screaming threats that he was going to kill them. Unfortunately for Alex, he did not have a big enough presence to scare or deter them in any way. Rather, it made his tormentors laugh all the more and just gave them more material to work with.

The effects of this bullying on Alex were beginning to be noticed by some of his teachers. They reported that he was reacting to different situations in a rather bizarre manner. When this was drawn to my attention I called Alex in for a chat. Alex at first was hesitant to acknowledge that he had a problem that was too difficult for him to manage alone. When I enquired if there were some people giving him a hard time he was grateful for the opportunity to talk about it, but was very reluctant to give names and wanted a guarantee of confidentiality. I respected his feelings and pride and listened to his story. We talked about what he had done to try to solve the problem himself. We explored his feelings and the effects that this ongoing harassment was having on him. At this point the true indication of Alex's hurt and pain began to surface. He explained that he was feeling frustrated, angry, shamed, weak and helpless. Even when he tried to avoid them they somehow managed to find him. Together we explored how he was feeling about himself, and he explained that all this had drained his confidence and he was very unhappy. He conveyed strong feelings connected to a time when they made him so angry that he had really wanted to kill them. It was affecting his ability to concentrate and work in class and he was on edge even when they were not around. Alex agreed that enough was enough and it had to stop, but he didn't know how to stop it.

We then began to explore what we could do together to overcome the problem. He finally acknowledged that he could do with some help. As a part of this I outlined the *shared responsibility* method in beating bullying. Alex was concerned that if others thought he had dobbed, things would get even worse for him. Dobbing was the worst thing a student could do. Dobbing has somehow become number one on the list of 'don'ts' in the students' unwritten 'code of ethics'.

Finally Alex mustered enough courage to take a risk and surrender the names of his three tormentors. He thought the *shared responsibility* method was the best plan of attack, but I think he was at the stage where he would have tried just about anything.

When I learned the names of Alex's tormentors my immediate reaction was, 'This might be more difficult than I first expected.' The boys were known to me, even though I had had very little direct dealings with them myself. The boys had a reputation of being uncooperative and less than helpful, particularly with their teachers. They were confident strong young men, often aggressive, very defensive, and mostly non-responsive to any staff wishes, instruction or direction, particularly when confronted. They were known to be very argumentative and rarely accepted any responsibility for their actions.

This was an excellent opportunity to further test the method. There was a temptation to speak to each of the boys individually as I knew how strong they could be as a group but I resisted this and arranged to meet them together. I followed the outlined procedures to the letter. I explained that I had been asked to catch up with Alex and he was a very unhappy person and this was worrying. I asked for their help in solving Alex's problem. I shared with them Alex's impact statement and talked to them about the wider effects of bullying. The boys were very attentive, cooperative and very eager to help. They shared some of the things they had said and done to Alex that they thought were funny, and explained how it all started at the camp. I was extremely encouraged by their maturity, openness, honesty, support and commitment to assist.

At the end of the day, the home group teacher of one of the boys made a special effort to find me. It turned out that this boy had spent quite a bit of his lunchtime talking with this teacher about our meeting and the impact it had had on him. 'I don't know what you did or said to Joel, but whatever it was it got through to him,' she reported. Joel had retold some of the general impact stories that I had shared with the group. He confessed to her that he had not stopped to think, nor did he have any idea of the possible impact and damage that the fun he and his mates were having at Alex's expense could potentially have on him.

The bullying stopped immediately and consistent follow-up over the following days and weeks confirmed an immediate, positive result for everyone. Alex reported feeling uneasy for a few days but confirmed no further bullying.

Dealing with the 'challenging' student may cause you to consider changing tack. My experience informs me—don't. When people have been treated with respect, not blamed, patiently taught and empowered to assist, they have revealed the valuable human qualities of compassion, empathy, responsibility and care.

CHAPTER THIRTEEN
STUDENT SUPPORT—THE 'WOUNDED' STUDENT

I was worried that without help she would find it difficult to reconnect with her peers and cope with future feelings of rejection or criticism.

By 'wounded' I'm referring to a student who as a result of bullying may display all or some of the listed symptoms. A wounded student may:
• be left with little or no sense of power,
• be left with little or no confidence,
• exhibit low self-esteem,
• be extremely nervous and find it difficult to look you in the eye,
• speak in whispers and use only a few words that you can hardly hear,
• be so scared and withdrawn that they avoid interaction with others,
• be suffering from isolation and rejection.

It is unreasonable to expect that a student who has been subjected to severe bullying can return to a school community and function well without support. To place a wounded student back into the school community without new skills, strategies and support could prove disastrous. This would simply be placing them at the mercy of every would-be bully in the school.

Bullying reduces a student's sense of power, confidence and self-esteem. In the next few chapters are useful basic strategies for assisting students as they overcome the effects of bullying and become stronger and safer at school. The ideas are simple, but effective. Anyone who possesses basic people skills should be able to implement them.

Supporting bullied students is primarily about 'empowerment'. All the suggestions and activities included here are intended to heal, equip, build up and empower students to rise above, as well as cope with bullying.

All students are different and possess different skills, interests and personalities. Bullying impacts on and affects students in diverse ways. The type and amount of support a student needs will depend largely on the individual, their degree of hurt, their natural skills, their personality and the circumstances they find themselves in.

Building a student up and inviting them to share in the responsibility is a good and non-threatening way to commence working with the wounded student. Involving the student in the process and the decision making is the beginning of restoration. It is helpful in the re-establishment of self-belief, power and confidence. This must be done with great sensitivity, as it is important that the student does not feel they are responsible for what has happened to them, or for solving the problem alone. Sometimes a wounded student can be left feeling they are to blame and there is something wrong with them. This can lead to self-hatred and more serious psychological problems.

When speaking with the student:
- affirm the student for his or her courage in speaking up,
- encourage the student to commit to ongoing support,
- let the student know they need to be in control and you are there to help them,
- involve the student in all decision making,
- seek the student's permission to act,
- encourage the student to be brave and be prepared to take a few risks and try new things.

Ask the student about places and activities outside school where they feel differently. This can be insightful and open many useful doors of opportunity. It is possible for a student to feel lonely and isolated at school but in their swimming club for example, they are happy, accepted and popular. Scouts, fire brigades, sporting clubs, youth groups, cadets, callisthenics and dance groups are among the many places where you might discover a totally different person exists.

If this is the case, explore the following:
- what is different for them in these other environments?
- why it is different for them?
- in what way do they *act* differently when they are there?
- in what way do they *feel* different?
- whether there is a connection between the way they act and the way they feel?
- how do people treat them differently in these other places?
- do they treat others differently?
- why do people treat them differently in these places?
- why is it they can be happy and join in the fun outside school and be so unhappy and isolated at school?
- how might they be able to bring these skills into the school setting?

Talk to the student about things they are good at. This can also be insightful and helpful in identifying any natural skills the student may possess. These skills can be channelled and prove useful in assisting a wounded student to recover and rise above the effects of bullying.

Confidence and power are often connected to a person's feeling of acceptance. Acceptance is often connected to a person's sense of confidence and power. Both are often connected to a person's abilities and successes.

Explore with the student:
- the things they are good at,
- the things they like to do,
- the feelings and confidence that are associated with doing things well,
- what happens to these feelings and confidence when they are at school and are being bullied,
- how they may learn to stand strong and protect their power.

Talk to the student about their relationships. This may reveal situations or relationships where a student possesses a degree of power, control and confidence. These skills, once identified, can also be channelled as a resource to assist a student to cope with bullying at school.

Explore the following with the student:
- relationships they have with friends, brothers and sisters,
- any sense of power, influence or control they may have in these relationships,
- what they would *do* if one of these people called them a name, or did something to them they didn't like,
- how they would *feel* if one of these people called them a name, or did something to them they didn't like,
- the reasons why these feelings are different to the feelings they experience when they are bullied at school,
- how the student may be able to bring these skills to school.

These points for discussion are not exhaustive. You need to work with the information given and set simple achievable goals that will build the student up and teach them new skills.

If you are unable to provide this support yourself, a referral to a counsellor or welfare person would be appropriate. Some schools run special small group programs designed to address these needs. One such program is called 'Friends' by Paula Barrett. It can be found at Friends for Life, Australian Academic Press, for more information see: www.australianacademicpress.com.au or www.friendsinfo. net

It is sometimes difficult to get a wounded student to commit to the extra support they need. A wounded student needs to be encouraged to share the responsibility in finding a solution to what is really 'their problem'. It is not in anyone's best interest for a student to expect the school to put a stop to the bullying while they themselves do not accept any responsibility for preventing it happening again.

Gemma was a shy, timid, 14-year-old Year 8 girl with limited social skills, poor self-esteem and very little confidence. She felt isolated and unwanted by a group of girls in her class who were ridiculing and making fun of her. Gemma sat silently with her head down as the girls mocked, laughed and made rude, derogatory comments about her work, personality and withdrawn nature. She became distressed and unable to cope. Gemma was an emotionally shattered, lonely and frightened young girl who spent a lot of her time in tears. Her parents had no idea how to help their daughter, other than contacting the school and demanding that action be taken against the girls involved. I arranged for the parents to bring Gemma into school, as she was not attending at that time and had not been for over a week. It took a few days for her parents to get her to agree to come. I requested that the meeting be held at the school, as I believed it was important in assisting Gemma to face up to and overcome her fears. I was prepared to do a home visit, but in the end it wasn't needed.

Gemma's parents were as hurt and upset by all this as she was. They were angry, aggressive, confronting, fighting hard to protect their daughter and needing desperately to find a way to ease her pain and suffering. Gemma was responding differently. She was wounded, withdrawn, running away, fearful and passive. Gemma sat quietly throughout the meeting, staring at the floor. When she did speak, she only used a few words at a time, and it was very difficult to hear her. Her parents were doing most of the talking. Most of the information I obtained about the impact the bullying was having on Gemma came via her parents.

'She just won't come to school any more.'

'She is scared, miserable and won't stop crying.'

'She spends most of her time in her room just lying on her bed sobbing.'

'She doesn't have any friends.'

'She won't talk about it and we don't know what to do.'

'It's taken us this long to find out what we have.'

Her parents' efforts did not appear to be helping Gemma at all. They made it clear: 'If the school can't fix the problem, then we will.' I don't know what they would have done and fortunately we didn't need to find out. I outlined the *shared responsibility* method the school was using in overcoming bullying and explained how effective it had been. I asked them what they would like to happen and what their desired outcome would be.

'We want to put an end to this and we believe the bullying students should be held accountable and punished.'

By this time Gemma's parents were beginning to calm down and could see that their approach was unlikely to help Gemma feel either better or safer, or assist in her return to school.

What they really wanted was a happy daughter, one who would attend school, one who would be safe and feel safe at school, and one who could learn without intimidation and ridicule. We all agreed on the objectives.

Gemma was being cared for and her parents could see this. They hesitantly agreed to allow the school to try and solve the problem through a *shared responsibility* meeting, but not without a further threat: 'If the school doesn't fix it, then I tell you, we will.' I wanted to know how Gemma felt about all this. I needed her permission to allow me to assist her in solving the problem. She needed to share in the responsibility and be involved in the decision making. She nervously whispered, 'I suppose it's all right.' I informed her that we would never know if it was successful unless she was prepared to help us by returning to school. This was the first step for her sharing the responsibility in finding a solution. Her parents interrupted by saying 'Don't worry, we will get her here.' I needed to hear it from her. Gemma's parents decided to keep her home for few more days to give the school adequate time to arrange and conduct the *shared responsibility* meeting before she returned to school.

I recommended that Gemma have ongoing support to assist in her recovery and equip her for her return to the school community. I was worried that without help she would find it difficult to reconnect with her peers and cope with future feelings of rejection or criticism. Her parents agreed that it would be beneficial. Gemma herself was silently reluctant and later through her parents expressed that she didn't need any further counselling and things would be all right once the bullying had stopped. I insisted that she meet with me at least once so I could explain how the support would be helpful, and why we recommended it. I had also arranged for a few helpful willing students to meet her, in an effort to make her transition back into school more comfortable.

On her return to school Gemma nervously attended this one appointment with me. Her body language was weak and her confidence was low. She listened without participating or committing to anything. Later, through her parents, I was informed that she had decided not to follow through with the counselling offer. Over the next few weeks I found it difficult to get any information from Gemma. I needed to know if the *shared responsibility* meeting had been successful, if she was OK, and if the bullying had stopped. Gemma was reluctant to say anything and I found it necessary to ring her parents a number of times to confirm the bullying had ceased. They were happy with the school and how we had managed the bullying problem, but they still expressed concern about Gemma's general unhappiness and lack of self-worth.

I took the opportunity to observe Gemma and her peers in class, as well as in the yard. Gemma quietly hung off the edge of the group without much involvement. The students who assisted her in her return to school were trying hard to include her and fussed over her a little.

The *shared responsibility* meeting had been successful, but even though the bullying had stopped, Gemma's self-esteem, confidence, friendship and social skills were so damaged or underdeveloped that her feelings of isolation and unhappiness continued. She didn't know how to fit in, belong or have fun. She was suspicious of everyone and dependent upon constant inclusion, fuss and to some degree, pampering. When others fussed or went out of their way to include her, she was happy, but if she was ignored, overlooked or forgotten, she was miserable. After a while Gemma realised her need of further support and attended two sessions. These sessions proved helpful but were not enough to uncover her full potential and completely get on top of the problem. Gemma did grow a little in confidence, and she did learn some basic friendship skills, but unfortunately she didn't accept the responsibility to see the process through.

Gemma's story is an example of students needing to share the responsibility in solving a problem. It does not help the student when they expect the school to put a stop to the bullying and do not accept any responsibility in preventing it happening again. Gemma is very likely to find herself in a similar position again.

I can't overstate the importance of the student being involved in the process and sharing the responsibility in achieving a positive outcome, even if it is in the smallest of ways. If the student is not involved, they can be left feeling even weaker and more helpless than before. Every time a decision is made or a task is completed the student grows a little more in confidence.

CHAPTER FOURTEEN

STUDENT SUPPORT—BODY LANGUAGE

If you look strong, you will begin to feel strong.

One of the most effective and immediate methods of empowering students to rise above bullying has been addressing negative body language. Encouraging students to become aware of their bodies and the messages given out has helped many wounded and hurt students to be safe and feel safe.

Damian was a very unhappy and extremely unmotivated Year 7 student. He expressed a hatred of school and, in particular, his class. According to Damian, no one liked him and he hated them all. He had no motivation to work and chose to sit by himself with his head down and do nothing. His parents had split up and the tension between them left him feeling there was no one he could talk to, or who really cared. Damian wanted to change schools but was fearful of where he would end up and what he might find in a different, unfamiliar school. When I met Damian, he scored himself on a happiness scale as a 2/10.

Damian had started Year 7 with some motivation. At the start he had a few friends and school was an escape from the many tensions he knew at home. It wasn't long before Damian's so-called friends turned and began to use him as an object of fun. Damian found this difficult to handle. He was hurt and started to withdraw from his entire class group. At first he tried to concentrate on doing his work, pretending he didn't care, but it wasn't long before he gave up on everyone and everything, his work included. The more he withdrew the more isolated he became. The more isolated he became the more he was bullied. The more he was bullied the unhappier he was.

Negative feelings escalated within Damian so much that at one point he lashed out aggressively and physically attacked another student in his class. As a result of this Damian found himself being disciplined by his teacher.

I worked with Damian for about a term. Initially my support for him centred on exploring his feelings and helping him cope with his family situation. It wasn't long before I realised that Damian was also a recipient of bullying. We spent some time exploring his interests and identifying the positive skills he possessed. Damian was a Cadet and loved the activities this involved. At Cadets, Damian felt important, liked, respected, confident and happy. At school he was completely the opposite. The bullying had completely destroyed his confidence and self-esteem. The bullying issue was successfully and quickly dealt with using the *shared responsibility* method, but Damian still remained fearful, unmotivated, isolated, and felt unhappy and powerless.

After discovering the confidence and skills he possessed and displayed as a Cadet, it became a matter of drawing and building on these skills and assisting him as he put them into practice at school. Damian didn't know how to turn things around, to make friends, or reconnect to the group. My challenge was not only to ensure that he was safe, but also to help him to feel safe as well. Damian not only felt weak and vulnerable, he looked it. He avoided eye contact, his usual gaze was down and he stood and sat with slumped shoulders. He moved slowly with very little energy. He spoke softly and apologetically. He hardly ever looked at me when he was talking. Damian needed to discover the power of positive body language. Addressing body language is necessary in assisting many students to develop confidence and self-esteem. If you look strong, you will begin to feel strong.

The protective and empowering qualities of positive body language should not be underestimated. Students who present with strong, confident body language are rarely bullied. Students who bully don't normally pick on someone who looks strong and confident; on the contrary they choose someone who looks timid, weak and lacking in confidence. A student who walks around the school with their head down looking at the ground and who avoids eye contact, whose shoulders are drooping and whose steps are lacking in energy, is a potential target for any student looking to climb the ladder of power within their peer group.

I have a newspaper picture on my office wall at school. The picture is of three AFL footballers after a game. They have their heads down, their shoulders are stooped and the picture screams defeat, humiliation, shame and weakness. I often use it to stimulate discussion and introduce the topic of body language to students. I ask students to explain how the footballers might be feeling. I ask the students, what would you say to them if you were their coach? I explain that the footballers would most likely be told to get their heads up and stand tall. They would be reminded of their skills and asked to consider what they have learned from the experience. In the end I suggest that the footballers are wearing suits or jeans and ask what may have happened to them? How do you know they are feeling bad? Their body language says it all.

Improving body language combats bullying on two fronts. On the first front it improves self-esteem, confidence and attracts friendship. On the second front it assists a student in being safe and feeling safe. If a person looks confident they begin to feel it and if they look and feel confident they are less likely to be bullied. Try walking around for a while just staring at the ground in front of you, hunch your shoulders, avoid eye contact, avoid conversation, walk in small lazy steps and I guarantee you will feel down and heavy, and it won't be one of your better days. Try walking around with your head up, a spring and energy in your step, make eye contact in a friendly manner, it's your birthday, take in the wider world, the blue sky, the gardens, the trees, etc. and I guarantee you will feel good and positive. The same results can be obtained regardless of whether you have contact with other people or not. However, during the second experiment you will find it difficult not to have contact with others because your body language, sense of confidence, energy and fun invites and welcomes others into your world.

To assist a student in overcoming bullying, encourage them to consider the messages they are sending out through their body language. Help them to be aware of what they are saying about themselves to others through the way they present themselves. Simple role-plays are helpful in teaching this. Enter the room displaying poor, non-confident body language. Enter again displaying strong, confident body language and ask the student which one is more likely to be bullied. Then discuss why. Use extremes to emphasise your point but make it clear you are not mimicking them. They will be somewhere in between these two extremes.

Encourage the student to stand tall with feet firmly on the floor. Get them to imagine there are roots connecting them strongly to the floor, supplying strength, power and energy to their entire body. Encourage them to walk tall and keep their head up. Challenge them to enter into an experiment for a day. Get them to walk around with strength, head up, big shoulders, with some bounce and energy in their step and see how they feel tomorrow. Draw a mental picture for them that says they are happy, safe and everybody likes them. There are only friends out there. This is an easy and non-threatening experiment because it does not involve risks of confrontation, or any potential fear that may be associated with involving or needing others. No one even needs to know what they are trying. To prepare the student for this you may consider taking them for a 'power walk' around the school. Make them aware of how they are presenting. Get them to notice any reflections of themselves in windows as they pass by. Ask them how they think they look. Keep encouraging them to find energy, have big shoulders, keep their head up, and make friendly eye contact with anyone they pass. Teach them to ignore anyone who does not look back or respond in a friendly warm manner. Most people are friendly and nice. Follow the student up the next day. Often the student will present happier and a lot more confident even before addressing the bullying situation. For others it may take more time, patience and encouragement.

Along with the importance of standing strong, teach students how to use their eyes. Encourage eye contact as, like Damien, many students are in the habit of avoiding it. The eyes are the windows of the soul. They say a lot about us. Start by developing friendly eyes. These are confident eyes that welcome others into our world: eyes that say hello; eyes that express friendship and fun. They are the eyes that a person should use most of the time. When people avoid eye contact they block out everyone, even those who are potential friends. When a person is unhappy and lacking in confidence, they often look down at the little piece of ground in front of them. Recipients of bullying often do this in an effort to keep safe, believing that if they don't look, the bullies won't do or say anything to hurt them. This is rarely true as it is often interpreted by the bully as weakness and a surrendering of power.

After friendly eyes are established commence working on strong eyes. These are the eyes a person uses when someone says or does something they don't like. Get the student to open their eyes a little wider and develop an expression that says 'No, I don't like or accept that.' I often use the example of an experienced teacher who can get a talkative student to be quiet by just looking at them. This illustration can help a student understand and develop 'the look'. All of us need to be able to stand strong and look trouble in the eye with a strong *no*. Get the student to practise this where it is safe. Rehearse some simple assertive lines with them, such as:

'Not funny.'

'Are you trying to bully me? I'm not going to be bullied by you or anyone else.'

'I don't want trouble but if you keep doing that I'll have to do something about it.'

The next step in improving body language is addressing the use of the voice. Carefully thought out words, a strong tone and strength in the voice are essential. Having strong body language and a weak voice or apologetic words will not stop bullying. A student responding to bullying with 'What did I do?' is weak and indicates a surrendering of power. Teach the students the difference between aggression and assertion. I usually point out that both are strong. Aggression involves attacking the other person either physically or verbally and is most likely to provoke a defensive or aggressive response. An assertive response is standing strong, saying you do not like something and won't put up with it, using words that do not attack or put the other person down. It is less likely to provoke an aggressive response. Teach them not to be apologetic or justify their existence.

Aggressive responses would include statements such as:

'You idiot, if you do that again I'll punch your head in.'

'Moron. You're dead meat.'

Assertive responses would include statements such as:

'Think twice before you take my stuff. It would be nice if you asked.'

'No, if you want something from the canteen you are quite capable of getting it yourself.'

'If you need money, ask your teacher, I'm not a bank.'

Encourage strong eye contact as well as good voice tone. Teach the student to keep eye contact for three seconds with head up, and looking strong before walking away. It is important not to surrender any power. Sometimes it is helpful to talk about passive responses as well. Explore with the student how passive, aggressive and assertive responses may leave them feeling. A passive response may leave a person feeling timid, weak or used. An aggressive response may leave a person angry, scared or threatened. An assertive response may leave a person feeling good, strong and proud.

Teach them to walk away from conflict without surrendering any power or looking weak. Standing up for oneself by telling a teacher, is not weak. It takes courage; it is strong and needs to be done. It is weak to do nothing. 'Dobbing' is a term used by bullies to scare their victims into a sense of helplessness. Not only should a student speak up for themselves, they should be praised for doing so. This is assertive, strong and courageous.

Damian responded well to improving his body language. He was cautious, but over time became more and more prepared to take new risks. Exercises on positive body language and the use of his eyes and voice became a weekly practice. The skills and confidence that he expressed at Cadets were beginning to be further developed and used at school. Damian admitted that he was a totally different person at school to who he was at Cadets. Over time this was changing. The other problem Damian was experiencing was his inability to make and keep friends in his class. Part of this was due to the fact that he didn't want to any more. If he was going to reconnect, belong, and find happiness at school he had to take a few more risks and learn how to make friends and keep friends.

CHAPTER FIFTEEN

STUDENT SUPPORT—BUILDING SOCIAL CONFIDENCE

Deep down he wanted to be liked, accepted and belong.

I asked Damian to think of someone he liked. At first he could not think of anyone so we thought back to his primary school where he could remember someone. I explored with Damian what it was about this boy that he liked. Damian revealed that this boy:

- was friendly and nice,
- was fun to be with,
- talked, listened and shared a lot of things with him.

These three simple ingredients are present in all good friendships and form the foundation of helping students to learn how to make friends and keep friends. It is not difficult to draw these three ingredients out of any student. They may use different words but all three are usually present. If not, explore a little deeper with them and fill in the gaps.

Emphasise and illustrate the importance of all three ingredients by taking the student through an exercise that leaves one ingredient out at a time. In the first illustration acknowledge the difficulty experienced in a friendship with a person who is fun, shares and listens, but is not always friendly and nice. For example, a student may treat another student differently when certain others are around.

A student may treat another student as a friend one day and the next they don't want to know them. A student may break or hide another student's property, or make fun of them in front of others. Anyone can see that such things will not produce a good friendship.

In the second illustration acknowledge the difficulty when fun is the missing ingredient in a friendship. Fun is particularly important for teenagers and children. All people need to be able to laugh, enjoy life and have fun together. A person who is friendly and nice, talks, listens and shows interest in others, but is always down, unhappy and reluctant to join in any games, activities or laughter, is often left out and is considered by others to be boring. Such a person is not fun to be with and often finds they are lonely and overlooked. It is important for a healthy friendship to include some fun. I acknowledge that it is difficult for a student who has been the recipient of bullying to feel happy and want to join in the fun. However, this must be turned around and the student encouraged to take a few risks and have a go. The longer they are out of the group fun, the more they will be overlooked, forgotten and the friendship chasm widens. There are some students who have never learned to have fun and, because of this, they find themselves on the social outer throughout their entire school life.

Such students are more likely to be targeted by bullies. Support needs to be given to these students to teach them to have fun and connect with others. Sports such as netball, cricket, basketball, and activities such as dancing, callisthenics, horse riding, bike riding and youth groups are among the many possibilities that parents and support people may consider encouraging the student to undertake. It is worth trying to uncover and draw out a sense of humour. A sense of humour is very powerful in overcoming and coping with many difficult life challenges. Laughing has many healing qualities. If there is no fun in the relationship the friendship will not be healthy or survive. One bullied student laughed at me when I called him a name. He thought I was funny. This student has the potential to learn to laugh at the names his bullies throw at him and render them powerless in their attempts to wound him.

In the third illustration consider a person who is nice and friendly, is fun to be with, but unfortunately never listens or shows an interest in others. This type of person always talks about themselves, what they have, what they have done, and they quickly change the subject if they are not the centre of attention. Such a relationship rarely works as it causes a person to feel that their thoughts, feelings, interests and opinions are not important or valued. It also can leave a person feeling they are not important, liked or cared about. Relationships like this are not on equal terms, are not healthy and don't often last.

Being friendly and nice, joining in and having fun, and communicating by listening and sharing, are the three important ingredients that combine to make a friendship work. Of course there are other relevant ingredients such as common interests, trust, dependability, personality, and compatibility that contribute to making and keeping meaningful relationships, but the basic three are simple, helpful and sufficient in assisting students to connect and find a way to belong and be accepted by their peer group at school.

Encourage students to reflect and consider their strengths and weakness in these three areas.

- Are they friendly and nice?
- Do they know how to have fun and are they fun to be with?

- Do they engage in positive communication? Do they listen and show an interest in others? Do they share information about their own interests and activities?

In Damian's case he could see how he had ceased to be nice and friendly. He was blocking everyone and everything out, and he was no fun. The ingredients that were needed for him to be connected and accepted as a part of his class were being ignored without him being aware. His hurt, anger and hatred had built a barrier that was keeping him from what he really wanted and needed. Deep down he wanted to be liked, accepted and belong. Damian explored with me ways we could start to bring about positive change. He identified some students in his class he felt would be safe to work with. We started to practise making conversation. Engaging in meaningful relaxed conversation is a skill that needs developing in many students. Damian and I had many simulated conversations that were designed to help him connect with others. We imagined that we were in situations or places such as:

- sitting with a stranger while waiting at a bus stop,
- helping a new student feel welcome on their first day of school,
- being the new student at school and finding out what needs to be known,
- sitting with someone at the football.

We worked on developing listening skills by picking up on personal interests and common interests that may be introduced into a conversation. I would get Damian talking about his Cadets and keep the conversation going by showing genuine interest and sharing any relevant experiences of my own that fitted in. At times Damian didn't even know that we were engaging in conversation-making exercises, because things were flowing naturally. At one time I remember stopping and asking him if he realised what we were doing. He said 'Yes, we are talking about the Cadet camp I went on last weekend.' It was a little more difficult for Damian to pick up on the clues and develop the conversation naturally, but over time he improved.

Some of the topics or clues I encouraged him to listen for and develop were:

- where a person lives,
- the hobbies or sports they play,
- the sporting teams they follow, etc.,
- similar experiences or adventures.

He then had to explore and develop the topics more deeply. The aim for Damian was to:

- get me talking in a comfortable relaxed manner,
- convince me that he was genuinely interested in me and what I had to say,
- convince me he was friendly and nice and would be a good friend to have,

- pick up on any interest of mine that we had in common and then contribute to the conversation,
- use open-ended questions to keep the conversation flowing and gain more information,
- get to a point in the conversation where it became natural and genuine, forgetting that we were in an exercise.

Over the term I worked with Damian sharing the responsibility in overcoming his bullying problem, his body language became stronger and more positive. He made and renewed many friendships. His sense of wellbeing, self-esteem and confidence grew. His social skills improved and he became happier both at school and particularly in his class. He no longer saw himself as being at the bottom of the social ladder. He now likes being in his class even though he says there are a few students in there who are not his type of person. He informed me he feels safe at school and very little bothers him any more. He participates well in class and his schoolwork is of a good standard. The bullying is a thing of the past and he feels equipped and confident to deal with whatever comes his way. Nowadays, I only see Damian when we pass in the yard. Before I included this story, I called him in to seek his permission and see if I had it all correct. He nodded his head in approval and said, 'Yes, that's pretty accurate.' At that time he reported being 8–9/10 on the happiness scale, a significant improvement on the 2/10 he rated himself when I first met him ten weeks earlier. Damian is living proof that the *shared responsibility* method is powerful and effective.

I realise that not all people dealing with bullying issues will have the training, skills or the time to provide the ongoing counselling support that is needed for students like Damian. I have deliberately kept things simple so people who would like to, and do have the time, can have a go. Those of you who are trained and experienced counsellors will have extra ideas and techniques that will further enhance and assist students to recover and equip them for the schoolyard. In some schools the *shared responsibility* meeting may be allocated to selected staff members and the welfare support aspects may be referred to others such as the school counsellor, youth worker or other support staff available. It is important that the support staff be familiar with the overall *shared responsibility* method and know what their role and objectives are in dealing with the recipients of bullying. Some schools might establish support groups or short programs that assist students in developing the confidence and skills they need. Not all students will need ongoing support and the amount of support required will depend on the individual student.

CHAPTER SIXTEEN

STUDENT SUPPORT—THE 'VICTIM' STUDENT

Above all else, do not show your fear.

By 'victim' I am referring to those students who by their very nature, appearance, personality, and presentation, attract negative, hurtful, bullying behaviours. It appears that some students are born with 'victim' tattooed on their foreheads, or 'kick me' pinned on their backs.

The type of support needed by the victims of bullying can be as different as their many faces. In this chapter I will share some techniques and ideas that have proven useful in assisting the victim student. Many of the techniques suggested in the previous chapters are helpful to the victim student, particularly the body language and friendship material. Not all victim students fall into the category of the wounded student but these students still require assistance in learning how to cope and be safe in the schoolyard.

Tim was not a wounded student but was being constantly picked on and made fun of. He was referred to the school youth worker because the school felt he could do with some support. Tim had trouble making friends, became angry easily, was often by himself, and was subjected to frequent teasing. Tim had poor body language, was not sporty or trendy and when he wasn't being ignored he was an object of fun and ridicule. The youth worker was given the basic information but the main objectives for the referral were never made clear. Tim was a typical victim student. The youth worker worked with Tim regularly for about three months. He explored his family life, his schoolwork, his interests, his feelings, his anger and his fears, and managed to assist Tim in many ways. Unfortunately, he did not teach Tim the skills he needed most. As a result, Tim continued to be a loner, feel unsafe, get angry easily and endure constant rejection and ridicule.

After dealing with the initial bullying issue schools are responsible for teaching the students:

- skills that will help them to be safe and feel safe at school,

- skills that will result in them being more resilient,
- how to stand strong and protect their sense of power,
- social skills in an effort to connect or reconnect them with their peers,
- skills that will help them build or restore their confidence and self-esteem,
- how to exist, survive and be safe in a competitive world.

Victim students often feed the bullying behaviours with their reactions. Temper outbursts are entertaining to the tormentors. Empty threats are amusing and pushed aside. Retaliations that get the victim student in trouble with teachers are points of gratification and power to the bullies. Ignoring bullying is hard to do and rarely works, unless it can be done really well. If whatever you do isn't working, change it.

Be prepared to explore and experiment with ideas that may be useful. It is here that the victim's story can be important as it reveals:

- what is happening,
- how they react,
- how it makes them feel,
- why it makes them feel the way they do.

Teach the student to block out hurtful words. Students are naturally good at blocking out words or choosing not to hear certain things. Teacher instructions are often not heard because the student's mind is far away in a more interesting place. Parent requests are often not heard because of selective deafness or self imposed immunity. Recipients of bullying, unfortunately, do not find it easy to apply this skill when tormented. They seem to need to tune in and listen to every little thing that the bullies are saying to them and about them. If students can block out their teachers and their parents they can learn to block out the bullies. What they do not hear or know cannot hurt them.

Get the students to go, to quote Happy Gilmour, to a 'happy place'. This is a place in their minds where they are happy, safe and engaged in doing something they love. *Happy Gilmour* is a silly light-hearted film but contains some valuable truths (*Happy Gilmour,* Universal Studios 1996). If you are familiar with the film talk to the students about it. Explore with them the impacts and effects Happy Gilmour's temper had on him, his life and the people around him, both the ones he loved and the ones he didn't.

I often get students to call me names for thirty seconds in a challenge to upset me. I spend those thirty seconds mentally planning what I need to do next or reliving one of my football or cricket triumphs. Many students find it difficult to call me names but those who have a genuine go, usually stop well short of the thirty seconds. We discuss how they felt calling me names and why the names didn't hurt me. Normally they say they felt stupid or dumb and acknowledge that I wasn't listening. I explain to them that this is not 'doing nothing', it is a deliberate tactic of 'self distraction'. With the students who respond to this I will have a go at calling them some names and insulting them. This I do with their permission and avoid any names I know they are sensitive to. In this situation students find it hard not to listen and often find it funny and start to laugh. Encourage the students to block out everything else and simply not to listen.

The ability to laugh opens the door for the development of 'deflection skills'. Why do students find it funny when I call them a hurtful and offensive name but get upset when others do the same? Craig was a Year 7 boy who was sensitive to many things. Craig would often cry and scream 'Why do they do this to me?' One of Craig's pet hates was having his path deliberately blocked by another student. If Craig tried to walk around they would move sideways to block him. This would cause Craig great distress and he would nearly always end up in tears. This activity became a popular game at school and it caught on quickly: 'Watch me make Craig cry.' I arranged to meet with Craig at lunchtime making sure I arrived before he did. When he arrived I opened the door and deliberately stood in his entrance path. Craig went to walk around me, so I responded by making it more difficult for him to get in. It didn't take long before Craig unknowingly engaged in a little game of cat and mouse. He playfully dodged, weaved, turned this way and that, and ended up finding a way in by crawling through my legs. He bounced around proudly proclaiming victory, bragging of his conquest. I asked him: 'What did I just do?' It took him a while to realise that I was doing exactly the same thing that had been upsetting him for a long time. Why did he laugh and play with me, but cry and freak out when others did the same thing?

It is possible to change the mindset of the students and teach them to join in the fun and deflect any bullying attempts by laughing at them. If a student possesses a sense of humour it is a valuable asset. Learning to laugh at ourselves and with others is important. We all do goofy embarrassing things at times and others are quick to pick up on them. If we learn to lighten up and laugh at ourselves it takes the sting out of a situation when others laugh or make fun of us. I will be the first to admit that some things are just not funny and cannot be laughed at, but some things are and can be. Learning to laugh is another positive aspect of making friends and is connected with our ability to have fun. Rather than be embarrassed about our differences we should learn to accept them. It is our differences that make us unique and state who we are.

Many people have made good friends simply by accepting a nickname that they have been branded with, others have become isolated by taking offence or showing hurt. One boy I knew was happy for his selected friends to call him 'Porka' but most upset when others did. This boy was actually excluding others with his own prejudice. If it was all right for some people to call him 'Porka' it should be all right for everyone.

Constantly work on identifying the normal reactions of students to everyday situations and if they are not working, try something else. Many situations of bullying have been avoided or overcome by light-hearted deflection.

'You're gay.'

'Who told you? They promised they wouldn't tell.'

'Hey Porky, you're fat!'

'This boy is quick, ten points for observation. Be careful I don't fall on you.'

'Hey girly.'

'You think this is cute, you should see me in a dress.'

These responses should be rehearsed, as they need to be delivered in a fun, light-hearted, non-aggressive, non-offensive, non-antagonistic way. Many of the funniest and best responses come from the students themselves. They just need a comfortable, relaxed atmosphere to think of them. Unfortunately, there are some students who just don't have the ability to laugh and make light of what is for them, a non-laughing matter. These students should be encouraged to look at other methods of overcoming the effects of bullying.

Drama is another strategy that has helped many students overcome the effects of being bullied. If I can't laugh things off easily, then I can pretend I can. If I can't get to the stage of believing that things don't bother me, then I can pretend I have. Talk to the students about the importance of acting positively and remaining engaged in an activity when someone has made an attempt to bully them. Bullies feed off reactions. Many students have tried to convince me that they have effectively ignored a bully only to find out they are still surrendering power unknowingly.

Aaron was a part of a group conversation when another student directed a bullying remark in his direction: 'And so what did you do "goop", have a cry?'

Aaron made every effort to ignore the comment but without realising it he surrendered power by his reaction. Aaron believed he didn't do anything, but he did. Aaron showed his hurt by his withdrawal from the conversation. He became a silent participant and hung as if wounded off the edge of the group. This is not effective ignoring. Students need to learn how to let the comment pass by without showing any signs of hurt or impact.

They need to adopt one of the following strategies:

- totally ignore the comment, then re-engage,
- give a strong glance of disapproval in the direction of the speaker, then re-engage,
- give an assertive statement of disapproval, then re-engage,
- deflect with humour, then re-engage.

The key is to remain engaged or to re-engage quickly. This is another form of deflection. Assist the students by showing ways in which they can do this. They can do this by directing a question at someone in the group, or by making a statement about the topic of conversation in a way that suggests they were not hurt at all by the comment.

A group might be discussing a football match played last weekend when a bullying comment is made.

'What would you know about football Smiffy. Girls don't play football.'

A light-hearted response might be, 'Yes I do. Anyway Hirdy's a girl and he plays. Are there any girls in your team Nick?'

(It is important not to engage the bullying student in the conversation or continue with his topic.)

If Smiffy can't laugh it off, then he may let it pass by without a response, but he must make an effort to remain or take part in the conversation.

Smiffy might add, 'Hey Barry, how was that goal Tarrant kicked in the third quarter?'

Smiffy may make strong eye contact with the student attempting to bully but just long enough to convey 'not funny' before re-engaging in the conversation.

'Hammo, now what was I saying? Oh yes, that umpire's decision at the end of the game…'

Smiffy may make an assertive comment before re-engaging in the conversation such as:

'Not funny. You'd do better to keep your comments to yourself, or direct them at someone who will appreciate them. Hammo, now what was I saying? Oh yes, that umpire's decision at the end of the game…'

If the bullying occurs in a class activity it is important that the student keeps socially engaged and does not become isolated. Bullying is most effective when it manages to isolate a victim from his or her group. Every effort must be made to stay connected without appearing wounded or surrendering any power.

If a student is going to cop it, teach them to cop it with dignity. I often talk about the movie scenario where a tough hero has all the odds stacked against him. He finds himself a captive to a group of thugs. He is being held back by a man on either arm while a tough gangster type guy punches him in the stomach and face. The hero struggles to get free and fight back, but he can't. He is a helpless captive. He, however, suffers with dignity. He keeps his head up and looks his assailants in the eyes with a look that says, 'You can break my body, but you can't break my spirit.' He bleeds with dignity, he surrenders no power and he stands strong.

Bullying is about breaking a person's spirit, it strips a person of their worth, power and self-esteem. Power and self-respect is a condition of the mind and should be kept at all cost. 'What if they hit me?' What if they do? What is worse, suffering in fear and feeling small, or getting a sore nose and bleeding with dignity? Your nose will be better in a few days but a broken spirit may never heal. The bully will then be faced with the consequences of their actions. My experience informs me that very few bullies will get to the point of hitting. They choose victims who they believe can't defend themselves. This is the nature of the bully. Bullies are mostly cowards. When a person's reactions and responses give the strong message 'no way', there is a good chance the bully will look for someone else to bully.

If a person can't stop the bullying on their own, they are entitled to get help. They should be encouraged to do whatever it takes to have the bullying stopped. This is not weakness, it is showing strength. Remind the student of the *shared responsibility* meeting method in beating bullying and how effective it has been.

These are all tactics you can teach students to help them to keep safe and protect their power. My advice to all students is to stand strong, look strong, stay engaged and above all else, do not show your fear. Students need to share in the responsibility for their own wellbeing and take a few risks. If something doesn't work, then try something else. Every time there is a success the student grows a little more in skill and confidence. Whatever the task you set, be gentle and encouraging. Start small. Experiment with power situations that are less threatening and build up to the more challenging ones. Make suggestions but don't advise. If something is too hard, back off a little. If someone tries and fails, encourage and praise the student for their effort. 'It took a lot of courage just to try, well done.'

CHAPTER SEVENTEEN
STUDENT SUPPORT—THE 'SKILLED' RECIPIENT

This is starting to really annoy me. Not funny any more!

Some students present more angry and annoyed than distressed or isolated when being bullied. They are not wounded students nor are they victim students. They walk, talk and present confidently. They explain the situation with controlled emotions and have no problems in talking with a teacher. They can explain what they have tried and they are willing and appear capable of trying assertive skills to overcome the situation. They have become annoyed and just don't know what to do other than landing in a fight. Skilled recipients usually don't fear the bullies. They simply have had enough. Many skilled recipients elect to engage the *shared responsibility* meeting in dealing with the bullying issue, but do not need further or ongoing support. Once the particular issue has been dealt with they are fine. They exist within the school community without fear or feelings of isolation. For others, providing some new strategies and empowering them to respond and overcome the bullying is often the best option. Many of the strategies outlined in the previous chapters can prove useful for the skilled recipient.

Teach and rehearse some assertive responses such as: 'I don't want trouble, but if you continue to try and bully me, I'll have to do something about it', or 'This is starting to really annoy me. Not funny any more!'

Another response that has proven effective is a strong, firm, *stop* or *no*: 'I'm not going to be bullied by you or anyone else for that matter. Find someone else to bully'. This becomes even more powerful when accompanied by a strong *stop* hand signal. Practise saying it with and without the hand signal and discuss the difference. Model for the students how these things can be said.

Statements such as these need to be rehearsed and delivered with conviction or they will be laughed off. You should gain a good idea as to whether the student has the capability to deliver them effectively. If you detect any nervousness or fear, gently discourage the student from this path. If there is a risk to be taken, let the student decide and point out that if this doesn't work the *shared responsibility* meeting can still be implemented.

A skilled recipient may decide to confront his tormentor and talk the matter through. If this is the case it is important that they don't confront the group. There is little chance the tormentor will back down or lose face in the presence of his or her supporters. The numbers and the power will be strongly against the skilled recipient in this setting. On the other hand, away from the group, the tormentor has less to lose and is more likely to listen and assist. The recipient may need some assistance in arranging to meet and talk privately with the tormentors. Talk through with the student what they want to say, and the best way to say it. Teach the student the difference between assertive and aggressive approaches. People do respect courage and strength, and an assertive response gives a clear message: 'I can and will defend myself. I am strong'. You may suggest the recipient says something like this:

> Warren, I have asked that you be taken out of class because I needed some private space to talk to you. I have been getting annoyed a lot lately, even angry. You may not have realised this and you may be just mucking around, but I'm not sure. What I wanted to say to you is that I don't want trouble, I don't want to fight, I don't want you in trouble, and I am hoping we can sort things out before things get worse. I want to know, do you have a problem with me? All I want is to be treated fairly and left alone. What do you think? We used to get on fine, what's happened? I hope we can sort things out but if we can't I'm going to have to take things further. I wanted the chance to talk with you first.

Another method of helping students, particularly boys, has been to utilise some of the material I gleaned from the *Rock and Water*[4] course I completed a few years ago. The purpose of this course is to teach self-control and help develop self-confidence. Activities are built around simple self-defence exercises that teach the importance of retaining balance and defending oneself. These activities have been extremely empowering.

Chinese Boxing is quick, fun and easy. It involves two people facing each other about a metre apart. They place their hands out in front at shoulder level with their

---

[4] *Rock and Water*: The Men and Boys Program by Freerk Ykema, The Family Action Centre, The University of Newcastle, Callaghan, NSW 2308.

palms facing out. They stand with feet apart at about shoulder width and engage in hitting each other's hands. The objectives of the game are to keep balance and knock the other person off balance by getting them to move their feet. There are two ways to score. The first is in attacking, that is hitting with enough force to cause the opponent to lose balance and stumble backwards. The second is in using the strength of the opponent, causing them to miss in an attempt to attack, resulting in their over-balancing and stumbling forward. If a person can get their opponent off balance to the point of moving a foot they score a point. A competition to five should only take a few minutes.

It is fun and very useful particularly in dealing with boys who are prone to losing control or getting angry. The skill of retaining balance is improved as a student learns how to attack and defend by taking the impact in their knees like the suspension on a car. Locked knees make it harder to retain balance. A student should be encouraged to find and keep their 'centre'. This is the point of balance in both attacking and defending. As I usually take the role of the opposition, I explain the activity and seek permission to engage in it with the student. This activity is not as much about winning as it is about balance and self-control. The spirit of competition adds to the fun. It is OK to let the students win but don't make it too obvious.

The most powerful aspect of this game is in drawing a parallel between the importance of physical balance and control, with that of mental and emotional balance and control. If a bully can make a student:

- feel weak,
- feel upset,
- surrender power,
- get angry to the point of lashing out,

then the bully has won a point on each count. On the other hand if a bully can't make a student feel either weak, upset, powerless or angry then the student has won.

A student learns to stay balanced and in control. We cannot control the actions of others but we must learn to control, and be responsible for, our own actions. This activity can be repeated over a number of sessions if a student is responsive and is benefiting from it. I often remind the boys that to be a man you need to be in control. Self-control is the beginning of power. I sometimes keep a score chart on my wall or get the students to keep a record of points won and lost over a week as an incentive. I may even offer a little reward from time to time.

Blocking exercises

Simple blocking exercises have also proven helpful in empowering boys. Most boys when wanting to start a fight do so by pushing the other in the chest. It appears that they are trying to provoke the person they are pushing into throwing the first punch. This is getting a little away from bullying, but its value is not so much in the exercise as it is in the confidence it builds. This confidence has proven very useful in helping students recover and making them safe and feeling safe.

There are four simple moves to learn in these blocking exercises. Explain to the student that they are going to be pushed four times. With each push they learn a different response.

1. On the first push, the pusher must feel resistance and strength. Teach the student to stand strong and balanced. Push them gently, with permission, on the shoulders, arms and chest and encourage more strength. When you feel strength congratulate them and tell them 'that's strong, good'. People respond to encouragement and try even harder. If a person feels weak when pushed it gives an extra feeling of power to the pusher. If they feel resistance and strength it gives them something else to think about.

2. On the second push, the receiver twists sideways, taking the pushed shoulder backwards to avoid contact thus causing the pusher to stumble slightly forward. The receiver must retain balance and eye contact and not move their feet. Many students turn their head with their shoulder and lose eye contact. Work to overcome this. Practise with both shoulders and encourage the student to be alert and take note of the attacker's preferred hand.

3. On the third push, the receiver blocks the push by bringing his arm with a clenched fist up on the inside of the pushing arm and forcing it to a line outside his shoulders. This should be practised slowly with both hands. The hand should move with strength and quickly as if suddenly released from a tensioned spring. On completion of the block the student's hand should remain up in a strong position. The same move can be used to block a punch. Balance and eye contact should be retained at all times.

4. On the fourth push the receiver disarms the attacker by combining steps two and three. This time when the shoulder is twisted, the blocking arm takes hold of the wrist pulling the pushing student further forward and off balance. This is the only move where the receiver moves his feet. As the receiver twists, he grabs the arm and pulls the attacker through while moving the inside foot a step backwards as he turns sideways. The grabbed arm is held firmly at the wrist and pulled upwards as the other arm is placed firmly on the shoulder-blade pushing down, holding the attacker in a powerless position. Balance is very important here.

These exercises can be practised weekly and the student can be encouraged to practise the moves with a trusted friend. Most students I have tried this with have loved it.

Points to remember:

- The starting position should always be one of balance and control. Physical and mental balance is a must.
- Avoid pacing, people pace when they are nervous. Pacing affects balance and alertness.
- Stand strong, head up, big shoulders, strong eyes.
- Breathe deeply; breathing becomes rapid and shallow when under threat, robbing the brain of much needed oxygen. A person needs to be able to think clearly. 'I can handle this.'
- Stand still with feet shoulder-width apart and knees slightly bent to absorb any impact.
- Stand at a distance of about two metres away from the attacker. This is a safe and comfortable distance, out of reach of any sudden unexpected movements. If any contact is to be made the attacker must move forward to reach, giving you time to respond. The movement forward assists in using the attacker's strength and momentum against him. Remain still and look the attacker in the eye. Keep the head up. Do not surrender any power.
- Keep things equal. If approached when sitting, stand up. Someone standing over you is commanding a position of power. Standing up equalises the power and puts you back on equal terms.
- Do not ask 'Why are you doing this?' or 'What have I done?' Both are statements that surrender power.

It is not my intention to encourage students to fight, but it is my intention to teach them to stand strong and not surrender any power to those who are intent on bullying. I cannot overstate the empowering benefits of these exercises. A few students have been so motivated by these that they have taken up self-defence as a serious interest. The power is not so much in using the skills, but in knowing and believing you can.

Peer mediation

Peer mediation is another powerful tool for schools. I believe it is always better to teach and empower people to confront and solve a problem themselves if they can. Assist by all means, but empower and involve the students in the process. This is what education and life is about. Mediation is more for conflict and *shared responsibility* is more for bullying. Conflict is where students are roughly of equal power and bullying has a strong power imbalance.

If a student lacks commitment to the line of action that should be taken it is sometimes helpful to ask:

'Have you had enough?'

'Is it time we put a stop to this?'

The examples of possible assertive responses mentioned above can and should be expanded to suit the language and culture of your school and the appropriate age level of the students involved. The student categories I have used in the last few chapters are of my own invention, and have been used solely to illustrate different needs and possible support strategies. They are not exhaustive, neither are the strategies. Many schools will have other, just as effective, strategies for helping bullied students.

...I'm bully proof

Meagan was a rather shy, nervous Year 8 student who lacked confidence and displayed limited social skills in knowing how to be accepted by her peers. Over the years I grew close to Meagan and came to know her quite well. Meagan often found herself the target of bullying behaviours because of her quiet and nervous demeanour. Her body language was poor and her presentation was one of a timid, rather weak young girl. One thing I admired about Meagan was that she always had a desire to learn how to overcome her problems and stand on her own two feet. She was open to self-improvement and developing skills that in turn would build her confidence and self-esteem. Meagan went through some rough times but always managed to grow and develop new skills and more confidence with each one. When Meagan began at our school she found herself close to the bottom on the student scale of popularity.

It was in Year 10 that Meagan found herself confronted with her biggest challenge of all in overcoming bullying. Meagan had a small but good group of friends. When Meagan gained a boyfriend, some of the 'popular kids' saw and seized an opportunity to bring her down. A group of three girls made it their business to ensure Meagan's romance was public knowledge. These girls continually bombarded her with embarrassing questions and statements about sexual activities and experimentation. They set her up as an object of humiliation and ridicule for the whole class to laugh at. Meagan fortunately only shared one class with this group and it wasn't long before this class became a very unpleasant and threatening place for her to be. Meagan found it difficult to deflect or respond to these vulgar attacks as well as the rumours that were spreading as a result of this bullying. It wasn't long before Meagan became totally isolated from the others in the class and unable to refrain from expressing her emotions openly. She needed to get out, she couldn't face it any more and it was too much for her to handle alone.

Meagan continued working with me developing her assertive skills and confidence. However, in facing this problem she felt the need to consider other plans of action and other avenues of support that may help. She had tried and wanted to be able to deal with this situation alone, but it was too difficult this time and she didn't know what to do. Meagan was aware of my work in overcoming bullying and the *shared responsibility* program. Out of desperation she finally agreed to let me speak to the girls. I outlined what I would do so she fully understood the process. The process was immediately successful and the bullying stopped and she was not bullied again.

I share this story not so much to illustrate the power and effectiveness of the *shared responsibility* method, but to give an example of a young girl who through support developed the skills and confidence to become bully proof and blossom towards realising her true potential. I pointed out to Meagan that in empowering us to assist her, she was in fact taking strong assertive action in responding to and overcoming her bullying problem herself. We don't need to do everything on our own. I continued to work with Meagan and support her on her life journey of growth and discovery.

When Meagan was in Year 12 she had risen to the position of School Captain. She served as a House Captain and as student representative on the School Council. Meagan was an active member of 'Youth Parliament' and also involved herself in many other causes and interests. Meagan was flying high. Her confidence, skills and assertiveness enabled her to stand in front of the entire school and lead assemblies.

On the bullying front Meagan declared in her own words, 'If someone tried to bully me now, it wouldn't bother me at all. I am bully proof!'

Meagan is working hard and enthusiastically towards realising her full potential, whatever that may be. She eventually experienced respect and came to realise what it means to be 'truly popular.' Her days of being bullied were over.

CHAPTER EIGHTEEN

A WHOLE SCHOOL APPROACH

Not all bullying behaviours need to be reported, but none should pass by unchallenged.

Shared responsibility is really much larger than just the *shared responsibility* meeting. It calls on all members of the school community to share the responsibility and be actively involved in making and keeping the school a safe place for all. Even though the *shared responsibility* meeting process is powerful and effective, the need to get and keep on top of bullying is much greater. A school needs to be *proactive* as well as *reactive* in beating bullying. The next few chapters outline some basic proactive ideas that have proven effective in engaging support.

Staff awareness and support

Keeping the anti-bullying issue alive and visible is important. Staff, in particular, need to be made aware and kept informed of the school bullying policy, procedures, events, surveys and developments. Selected staff should be trained and all staff should be familiar with the *shared responsibility* practice. Regular updates should be given to remind staff of what is happening and bring new staff up to speed. Survey results should be shared at staff meetings and staff encouraged to look out for particular behaviours. Identification of these behaviours should be accompanied by suggestions as to how staff might respond when they come across them in the yard or classroom.

'Naomi, name calling is bullying, we don't bully here. Now, what should you be doing?'

'Do you realise Peter that what you just said is bullying? We don't have bullying in this school. Now get back to your work.'

'Thomas, are you bullying? I hope not. Bring me your work so I can see where you are up to.'

'You may not have stopped to think about it Sarah, but deliberately excluding someone from your group is a form of bullying. Is that what you intended? You only have this period to finish this work so you better get on with it, together.'

I could write a whole chapter containing deflection statements that require little time, effort or fuss, but make a strong proclamation that bullying is not acceptable. Simple statements such as the ones listed above are skills that many staff need to develop as a part of their teaching practices.

Deflection statements:

- act as deterrents,
- put out little spot fires,
- remind the students that the staff are proactive and do not tolerate bullying,
- educate the students about bullying,
- protect the victim by drawing the attention away from them with minimal fuss,
- direct the would-be bully back to what they are supposed to be doing,
- keep the anti-bullying campaign alive.

Not all bullying behaviours need to be reported, but none should pass by unchallenged.

Place a box in the staff room in which teachers can place the names of students they believe are victims of bullying. Place a second box so staff can refer students who they know to be bullying others. Remind the staff regularly about the referral system and the purpose and placement of the boxes. It is best to have standard referral forms available with the boxes so the students can be easily followed up and the details uniformly recorded.

Curriculum involvement

Talk with curriculum managers about material and ways of incorporating the topic of bullying and conflict into the everyday curriculum. Book a place on their meeting agenda and speak to them about the seriousness and impact of bullying. Request their assistance in getting the issues and topics addressed within the various faculty levels. Topics and issues that relate to bullying or conflict can then be drawn out and further explored.

Support and team work

Get a welfare committee or a group of interested people together to brainstorm and plan activities and awareness strategies that can get, and keep, things going. This group could look at what the school is currently doing and how effective it is. They may evaluate the current school policy and procedures with a view to instigating positive change and/or improvements. Be careful not to throw out what is proven, good and works.

Drama and speakers

Organise a visiting drama group for a school camp, or plan for them to visit the school and present a program that engages the students in bullying awareness and a responsibility workshop. Unfortunately these can be expensive. Some schools may be able to utilise their own drama department and/or classes to achieve this.

Special focus

Look at having a bullying awareness week in your school, with guest speakers, competitions, films, etc. Do a feature on sexual and racial discrimination and harassment. This is another way of keeping the issue alive as well as educating and supporting our young people.

Visual awareness

Place anti-bullying posters in classrooms and other strategic places around the school to create a constant awareness that bullying is not acceptable, and is taken seriously by the school.

Regular articles or positive reports in relation to anti-bullying should be put in the school newsletter. Positive initiatives, survey reports, training activities, and issues such as 'Dobbing' and 'Why do people bully?' are good topics to include. Stories can be powerful in challenging negative viewpoints and empower parents and recipients to take action. Local newspapers can be valuable, but care needs to be taken to avoid journalistic sensationalism.

A few years ago I wrote an article for the school newsletter about the encouraging results of a student safety survey that confirmed the school was on the right track in combating and keeping on top of bullying. Of the Year 7 students, 94% reported that they felt safe at school. A local newspaper picked up on this article and contacted me for an interview. The Principal was proud of our achievements and thought the story would be good for the school. The paper was interested in what we were doing and was keen to use our school procedures and data in outlining what can be done to combat bullying in schools. The overall article was positive and pleasing. However, the first sentence of the article read, '6% of Year 7 students reported feeling unsafe at school'. This form of sensational journalism set a negative tone for the whole article. It would have been good to commence with, 'School proud of student safety records in keeping on top of bullying.' We were proud of what we had achieved. The article went on to disclose many positive achievements and initiatives that the school has implemented but the potential damage was done in the opening phrase. It might be best to get a copy of what they intend to print before they print it.

CHAPTER NINETEEN

A WHOLE SCHOOL APPROACH—SAFETY SURVEYS

I have found that providing an opportunity to name bullies has acted as a deterrent for those students who may believe they can continue to bully undetected.

Regular student safety surveys are also a good way of keeping on top of bullying and getting much needed, yet sometimes suppressed, information. The majority of bullying goes undetected, so schools need to be proactive in implementing safe and accurate methods of keeping in touch with student feelings and what is going on in their school. These surveys need to be anonymous and administered under very strict conditions so the data is pure and non-corrupted. (See Appendix One for an example.)

Surveys provide schools with data that can be compared from one year to the next. They provide information that can be used to evaluate how effective the program has been, as well as indicating what needs to be done to ensure further improvement. The 94% of Year 7 students feeling safe was a 3% improvement on the 91% from the previous year. In fact the results indicated that there had been significant improvement in all the areas addressed in the survey compared with the previous year.

The surveys should contain a map of the school where students can indicate what they consider to be unsafe areas. This is a positive way in which the school can identify and respond to problem areas.

The surveys should include gender and year level identification. Year level can be identified by simply colour coding the surveys. Some behaviour may be particularly gender specific and it is good to know this. Including gender also gives an indication of who is bullying who. Is the bullying basically confined within genders, or is it transcending them with boys bullying girls and vice versa?

The surveys should contain a list of common bullying behaviours and provide the opportunity for the students to indicate what is happening to them, and what they have seen happening to others. This allows the school to identify the most common types of bullying behaviours and address and respond to them accordingly. As a result of this information a school might have a focus week on clamping down on threats or extortion.

The surveys need to be quick, no longer than 10 minutes for the slowest working student. They should be 'tick the box' and 'mark the map' with the exception of the naming of the bullies. It should be administered by a teacher other than the normal class teacher and completed under test conditions. The students are not to be informed beforehand that it will take place. The teachers themselves should only be informed at the latest possible time. All the classes to be surveyed should be covered in one block, avoiding a break where students would have opportunity to talk, collaborate, plan or sabotage the result of the survey. A group of 6–8 teachers with strong disciplinary manner will cover up to 24 classes in about 90 minutes comfortably.

The class teacher should be used to help supervise and ensure test conditions. The survey is introduced by an administrator, reading from a prepared preamble (see Appendix One for an example).

The preamble states that:

- student safety is important and everyone in the school needs to work together to make this happen.
- the school is seeking student assistance in making and keeping the school a safe and happy place for all.
- there is to be no talking during the survey.
- no questions will be answered during the survey. If a student does not understand a question they are to leave it blank and go on to the next question. (Responding to questions, or conducting any form of conversation, impacts on concentration and an individual's thinking is influenced. This no-questions approach is essential if you want pure, non-corrupted data.)
- when a student completes the survey they are to sit in silence, close their survey, put their pen down and wait until everyone is finished.

The surveys should be collected before any talking is allowed. The class should be thanked for their help and the completed surveys returned to an agreed central position or person.

Seating plans and writing materials need to be organised before the survey is handed out and commenced. Any student who will not be quiet or is being uncooperative should be excluded and removed temporarily from the classroom while the others complete the survey. Integration students may have assistance from their support staff and if a passage way or adjacent room is near by then it should be made available to them. Sport classes and subject rooms where it is not practical to do a written survey should be avoided and taken into consideration when selecting a suitable time block to administer the survey.

The surveys may provide students with the opportunity to anonymously name other students who are bullying them, or they have witnessed bullying others. There has been some rigorous debate over this issue in recent years but I have found this information to be valuable, helpful and beneficial. However, in stating this, I need to point out that this particular information needs to be handled with great care and responded to only under very strict, agreed to, conditions. Schools should guarantee that no attempts will be made to trace information back to an individual student and no disciplinary action will be taken on the information obtained through the surveys alone. I have found that providing an opportunity to name bullies has acted as a deterrent for those students who may believe they can continue to bully undetected. As a rule, a student would need to be named a minimum of four times before follow-up is considered. The number of students taking part in the survey could be used as a guide to calculate the cut-off number. You would never follow up a student named once or even twice. Some students may name someone whom they are having a fight with at the time, or they simply don't like. Students named three times may be followed up, particularly if the number of survey participants is small, or all three students are from the same class. Students named four or more times should definitely be followed up.

The following up of students named as bullies in the surveys follows much the same format as a *shared responsibility* meeting. In this meeting there is no identified victim or impact statement, so the line of approach needs to be slightly different. The student's attention should be drawn to the recent safety survey and they should be made aware that a number of students in the school have indicated that they feel unsafe with them. The discussion and teaching about what bullying is and the potential impact it has should be included. General impact stories should be used to support this process. Students should be asked, 'What can you do to help solve the problem?'

The meeting information and outcome is to be recorded on the same Shared Responsibility Meeting Form (see Appendix One) and appropriately marked to indicate that the information was gained through a survey. These interviews can be done individually or as a group, but careful consideration needs to be made when deciding who makes up the various groups. If students are from the same class group, or you know they belong to the same social group, then it is easier. It is not advisable to group students together from different year levels, or who are unknown to each other.

When I did my first survey many years ago, I left it to the individual class teacher to administer at their convenience, with few guidelines. Although many classes returned some valuable data, others had obviously been allowed to talk and discuss the questions freely. These classes did not take the survey seriously and much of the data was corrupted. We had a number of Mickey Mouses and unpopular students or teachers set up and named as bullies. In the end it was decided that any survey with a dubious response anywhere on it, was to be considered corrupted and could not be used as reliable data.

The survey is best prepared on an A3 sheet that is then folded with the questions on the inside. The outside cover may have the name of the school and a title such as 'Shared Responsibility Students Safety Survey' on it (see Appendix One).

Schools will need to adapt the survey questions to suit their individual needs. Some years, more, or a different type of, data may be required. The advantage of keeping the same format is that data can be compared year to year more easily.

Surveying parents on their thoughts and feelings about bullying can also be valuable. As well as making them aware of the school's serious intent in keeping on top of bullying, it also has the potential to uncover incidents and gain much needed support.[5]

Bullying is an issue that unfortunately is ongoing. If the issue is forgotten, or neglected for a period of time it grows back quickly. Bullying awareness, education and intervention needs to be an active ongoing program in every school. Many schools have a strong awareness program but do not have an effective method of ensuring safety or changing the behaviours of the bullies. Other schools have an effective way of dealing with the bullies, but never get on top of it because they remain basically reactive and fail to be proactive.

---

[5] Survey information available from Ken Rigby
www.education.unisa.edu.au/bullying/questdescrip.htm

CHAPTER TWENTY

A WHOLE SCHOOL APPROACH—TEACHING IN THE CLASSROOM

All these things are bullying, and all these things are not bullying.

All teachers should be encouraged and constantly reminded that they should take every opportunity in the classroom to teach about bullying. It may be in response to certain comments or attitudes, and may be short and not necessarily a part of the planned curriculum. On the other hand there are many topics where aspects of relationships, social skills and community give rise to an opportunity to teach about bullying in a more structured way. Art and other drawing type activities might use 'bullying' or 'relationships' as a topic for design, posters or values expression. English and social studies subjects may debate, discuss, write about, evaluate, and explore the impact of such topics within the normal curriculum. Teachers could select books, films and/or include topics that keep the importance of social acceptance and behaviours in the forefront of the minds of their students.

Over the years I have received many invitations to take a lesson or a short series of lessons on relationships, friendships, social behaviours and particularly bullying. In most instances this has been 'after the horse has bolted'. It is usually that the social competitive struggle in a group has escalated to a level where the teacher has become very concerned about the manner in which the class members are relating to each other and, in particular, treating each other.

This can be a difficult challenge as, by this time, the power groups are often well established and their behaviours well entrenched. The ideal way of proactively addressing the bullying issue is best done as a part of a pastoral care type subject. In my first school in my capacity as chaplain I was given the opportunity to teach all the Year 7 students for the entire year about life and relationship skills. However, not all schools have chaplains or the staff who can teach such a subject, nor do they have the timetable space in an already busy competitive schedule.

One-off lessons, even though reactive rather than proactive, can still prove valuable and effective. Even a different face, a different presenter, can add to the impact the content can have on individual students. Some time ago I was sitting in my office catching up on some neglected administration when I received an internal phone call. It was a teacher who was currently working his way through a double Year 7 session. Apparently the frustration level of the teacher relating to the students' treatment of each other had risen to such a level that it was time to do something immediately about it. The invitation was extended to me to come and talk to the class about bullying in an effort to change the social dynamics of the group. I had nothing prepared but felt motivated enough to take the challenge and just run with it. I grabbed a whiteboard marker, a bullying survey sheet that was lying around and headed to the classroom.

On my way to the classroom I was throwing a few ideas around in my head as to how I might be able to adapt the successful *shared responsibility* meeting process to a classroom situation. The main issues that form the foundation of this method are welfare, education, discipline and the sharing of responsibility. There was no reason why this should not work and it could form the foundation of this lesson.

I was well aware that there were at least two targets of bullying in this class and I would need to be sensitive to their feelings and position. I was also conscious of the need that we all have to belong and have meaningful relationships or friendships. This challenged me to include the 'making and keeping friends' material that was proving successful in some of my counselling sessions.

I share this experience with you in the hope that it will prove useful or adaptable to some of my readers. After explaining why I was invited into their classroom, I introduced a discussion around the question 'What is important for a person to be happy and successful in life?' The students eagerly threw many ideas at me and I quickly listed them on the board. The list included all the expected answers, money, a good education, money, a good job, money, a host of material possessions, which included money, houses, cars, boats, etc.

I followed this up with another question. 'Is it possible to have all these things and still be unhappy?' The discussion progressed to a deeper level, to the recognition that all people have a need to be loved, to belong, to be accepted and recognised within their social groups. It is a basic human need. People need people. Money, possessions, position and power, although important, do not guarantee happiness or security. However, secure, meaningful, loving, caring relationships have helped many people through some very tough, difficult situations.

We then went on to discuss how our need to belong affects our behaviours, the way we talk, the way we walk, the things we will do and in some cases the things we won't do. I gave a few dramatic renditions of mannerisms and interesting behaviours of past students who were trying very hard for attention, popularity and social position. We acknowledged that there was nothing wrong with these desires, in fact they are healthy and are needed if we are to be happy and successful in life. People need a sense of power to develop self-esteem, confidence and to realise their potential. We want everyone to be happy and successful and as a community we really have a responsibility to assist each other in making our world a better place for everyone.

By this stage of the lesson any small signs of negativity or defensiveness had completely disappeared. I made the point that nearly everything we do in public is motivated or influenced by how others will see us, will like us, will accept us. We want and need to be accepted and liked, as well as feel we belong and are part of the fun. We like it when others think we are cool and funny. We like it when others listen and pay attention to us. We like it when others follow us and do what we say.

It adds to our sense of power and importance that is connected to our sense of belonging, acceptance and social position.

However, sometimes the means of getting this recognition can be hurtful and harmful to others without us even realising it. We can get so caught up in our need to belong, to be liked, to be popular, that we fail to notice or acknowledge that everyone else has need of the same things. Without thinking we can be hurting others in our efforts to be happy and belong. We don't have to be close friends with everyone but we do need to be accepting and respectful. We need to learn to acknowledge and respect difference. Include, don't exclude.

At this point of the lesson I introduced the topic of 'bullying' with the question, 'Is bullying a good thing or a bad thing?' The response to this question as I expected, was a unanimous 'bad thing'.

As I had done so many times before, I discussed why it was bad. From the class came statements and stories that could be likened to 'impact statements'. Anyone who was courageous enough to share a story was asked, 'How did this make you feel?' For a short moment we acknowledged the fact that for the bully, bullying can be a good thing. It gives them a feeling of power and what they believe to be respect. We acknowledged that hardcore bullies rarely have close friends who really trust and respect them. A lot of the young people who appear to support bullies do so out of a fear that they may also become their victim, or they are searching for their own sense of power and position on the back of the bully.

The topic was getting very serious and heavy. The lesson needed lightening up. There was still a need to challenge the students in other related areas. I engaged the class in a quick verbal survey with the assistance of the classroom teacher. I wrote a behaviour up on the board, 'name calling'. I asked the class to put up their hand if they thought this was bullying and recorded the number. I did the same for those who thought it wasn't. I did this quickly as possible but encouraged the students to give their own opinions, immediately, without looking towards their friends. We briefly discussed why it is important to know what others are thinking before we make known our own feelings and decisions. The class could see the truth, 'we all feel the need to belong, to be accepted, and this has an impact on our actions'. I encouraged the students to make their own decisions and pointed out the courage that was needed to do so. It takes a lot of confidence and courage to express our own beliefs, values, and feelings, without the fear of rejection or the ridicule of others. We need to respect difference and believe in ourselves.

I made no comments or judgements on the number of yes or no answers other than thanking and encouraging anyone who appeared courageous enough to express an opinion different to the group. I listed a number of other bullying behaviours such as:

- making fun of others,
- taking money,
- interfering with property,
- leaving others out,
- turning others against a person, etc.

I quickly registered the results on the board for all to see. I covered each bullying behaviour separately so as not to confuse the students or have them thinking about a number of different behaviours at the same time. The results were far from unanimous.

After this quick survey I made a statement: 'All these things are bullying, and all these things are not bullying.' I asked the question, 'Why?' This helped all the students to feel affirmed. No one likes to be told they are wrong and in this case they were all affirmed for being correct. The behaviour obviously depends greatly on the situation and the circumstances surrounding it.

Where appropriate, I gave everyday examples of the behaviours. I always started with the 'not bullying' example, and then followed up with the same behaviour as 'bullying'. I wanted the students to see clearly when a behaviour was bullying and when it was not. The intent has to be considered, but above all, the impact that the behaviour is having on the person is the true and main indicator:

- Is it helpful or is it hurtful?
- Is it inclusive or exclusive?
- Is it friendly or unfriendly?
- Can the person deal with it well or not?

We talked about name calling and when it is or isn't bullying. I shared the example of my friend and myself that I have included earlier in this book (see page 32). In some circumstances name calling can contribute to a good relationship, one that is accepting, warm, and friendly. In our situation our little name calling game gave birth to a lot of fun and mutual respect. On the other hand, if someone who didn't like me started calling me names and did so in a manner that made me feel uncomfortable, then it may be bullying. If they are aware of my discomfort and continue to use it, then it is most definitely bullying. If they are not intending to be friendly and accepting, or include me in the group, there can be no doubt that this is bullying. Bullying is ongoing behaviour that is not inclusive or respectful and is hurtful.

When can taking money from a person not be considered bullying? If I ask to borrow money from a friend and I intend to pay it back, then it really can't be considered bullying. But if I am waiting at the out door of the canteen watching to see who gets change and then ask them for the money that I know they have in their pocket, without any intention of paying it back, then it is bullying. It is actually worse, it is extortion and criminal. Sometimes students don't realise that what they are doing is bullying. They insist that the person gave them the money and they didn't demand it or threaten them at all. A further discussion as to why they selected that particular person can uncover their abuse of power and use of intimidation. They gave the money to them because they were scared not to, or they hoped they would be liked and be accepted into the bully's group. It's unlikely that giving a bully money will result in them accepting or liking someone.

Examples of all the other behaviours can be easily and quickly thought up. As a part of this lesson I engaged the class in exploring what makes a person a good friend. The three ingredients of friendship that I have outlined in Chapter 15 of this book were drawn out. They did not come forth in the same order, or with the same words, but they came out as:

- be friendly and nice,
- be fun and have fun,
- practise two-way sharing (listening as well as sharing).

Any two of these without the third does not amount to a good friendship. If these are the things we like in others, then we should look at ourselves to see what sort of a friend we make. We all like to be treated in a manner that is friendly and nice. We all need to have fun and be fun. We all need an outlet, someone who will listen to and is interested in us, as well as being prepared to listen to and show interest in others. So, am I friendly and nice? Am I fun to be with? Do I show an interest in and listen to others? Do I share things about myself with others who I can trust? Most people can honestly say that they are friends to some people and maybe not to others. Is there value in being friendly and nice to everyone, even those who are outside my immediate group of friends? We need to be respectful to everyone. I outlined to the class the various scenarios where one of the three might be excluded and then posed the question 'Is this a good friendship?'

The lesson finished with a discussion around why the school takes bullying so seriously. I wanted to make sure that all the students knew the school rules, the school policy and the support people they could talk to if needed. Every person who is a part of the school community has to share in the responsibility of making and keeping our school a safe and happy place for everyone.

I felt the lesson went well but was most encouraged later. Apparently, immediately after the lesson a group of boys approached a previously isolated student and invited him to be a part of their group. Another student reported a number of apologies and a newfound friendship group. The teacher reported a noticeable change in the way the group were interacting and the social feeling within the group. I can only hope it continued. A few students self-referred for skill development and confidence building— all positive stuff.

In the lesson I was careful not to talk about individuals or particular behaviours that I knew were occurring within the group. I did not include names, nor did I indicate in any way that I was aware of individual situations. It is important to keep the issues general and not run the risk of embarrassing anyone who may be feeling isolated or vulnerable. I was further encouraged to learn that a student, who had been withdrawn and isolated as a result of being bullied, was empowered by the lesson and took an active role in all the class discussions.

CHAPTER TWENTY-ONE
COMPLICATIONS AND WELL-MEANING PEOPLE

I'll tell you what to do. The next time he lays a hand on you, turn around quickly and plant one right between the eyes, as hard as you can.

Things are never straightforward when dealing with bullying issues. There are often many variables, expectations, ideas and imposed solutions to contend with. One complication that can cause the school concern is the well-meaning parent. This is the parent who gets involved and tries to solve the problem on their own. When they can't, they turn their aggression and frustration toward the school.

The most common advice the well-meaning parent gives their child, is to hit back. 'If anyone gives you a hard time I give you permission to bash them.' This advice is not often followed because most children who are bullied fear the bully and what the parent is asking is too hard. This well-meaning advice can further stress the already hurting student, as it has the potential to result in additional trauma, fear and isolation. The student most probably is experiencing feelings of embarrassment and shame associated with being bullied and they are complicated further with not being able to live up to the parent's expectations. The child becomes further isolated because they feel they can no longer talk to their parents about it.

Billy was being constantly teased and tormented by Gavin who, by all accounts, was the toughest kid in the class. Gavin had his group of friends and he worked hard to impress them. In sport Gavin would deliberately throw balls at Billy as hard as he could. He would take every opportunity available to bump into him and knock him to the ground. Even in games such as basketball and hockey he always found ways to assert his power and hurt Billy. Pushing Billy into the goal post, or deliberately hitting him in the shins with a hockey stick, were part of Gavin's weekly sporting activities. Whenever Billy was within striking distance Gavin struck him.

Billy was having a difficult time knowing what to do about this. Gavin was big and strong and Billy was small and puny. Physically Gavin was all Billy aspired to be.

Billy believed that if he told someone and Gavin got in trouble things would get worse, so he kept silent. When Billy's dad enquired about the bruises on his arms, he teased Billy about the need to keep his guard up and fight back. After a while his dad noticed that this was really upsetting Billy and maybe there was more to it than just harmless horseplay. Billy was happy to have the opportunity to talk to someone about it. 'Dad will know what to do; I am no longer on my own.' Billy told his dad about the punching, the bumping and what was happening in sport. He showed him other bruises that he had been hiding. His dad was rightfully concerned, 'What do you do when he hits you son?' Billy did not answer. He sat there staring at the kitchen floor. His dad adopted an angry, aggressive tone. 'I'll tell you what to do. The next time he lays a hand on you, turn around quickly and plant one right between the eyes, as hard as you can. That will make him think twice about touching you again. I don't care what the school says; you have a right to defend yourself.'

There was nothing that Billy would have liked to do more, but he knew it was only a dream. He had never been in a fight in his life. Gavin was scary and there was no way he could take him on, let alone beat him in a fight. Billy didn't want to show his fear or tell his dad he couldn't do it. He wanted his dad to be proud of him. Billy admired his dad. He possessed all the toughness and courage that he longed for. Every few days his dad would ask, 'Have you fixed that Gavin kid up yet?' Billy kept his bruises covered and lied to avoid disappointing his dad. Billy thought, 'I don't want dad to hate me, to be angry with me, or think I'm weak.' This 'well-meaning' dad did not help his son at all. He did nothing to address the problem other than push it further underground.

The young person being bullied needs support but what is advised and/or expected must be within their capabilities. Most students want to be able to look after themselves and solve their own problems. Being bullied often comes with feelings of helplessness, weakness, failure and self-hatred. The well-meaning parent tries to empower and protect their child by teaching them that violence is the answer. In reality, violence hasn't solved many problems at all. Even if a child does muster enough courage to hit back, the parent is teaching the child to deal with the problems in a very unhealthy way. The well-meaning parent often creates confusion for the child by contradicting the school rules. Schools cannot condone violence. What does a child think or learn when the school is issuing consequences for something that their parent told them to do? Parents can cause further confusion for their bullied child when the child fights back and hits a sibling at home and is punished for it. What values do we teach our children when there are obvious contradictions?

The problem can be further complicated when a parent receives notification that their bullied child is being suspended for fighting. The parent often tries to justify the action as retaliation and accuses the school of failing in their duty by not doing anything about the bullying problem in the first place. The question is, did the school know anything about the bullying problem in the first place? The parents of a bullied student have a right to be angry and expect a safe and supportive school environment for their child. However, the parents and the school need to work together and share the responsibility in ensuring this is provided, not only for their own child, but for all students. Giving advice that contradicts the school's policies and procedures will not achieve this goal. Schools are required by law to have policies and procedures in place and parents need to display confidence in the school when dealing with such issues. If the school fails to deliver then there are avenues to pursue.

There are many well-meaning parental statements that complicate bullying issues and make things more difficult for schools to manage. For example:

'Whatever they do to you, do it back to them, only harder.'

'If they bother you, hit first and ask questions later.'

'Find something they don't like, and pick on them.'

'Go get your brother, he'll fix them.'

'Take Joel with you, he doesn't tolerate any nonsense.'

'Tell them if they don't watch out, I'll come to school and they can deal with me.'

This last statement raises a further complication. It occurs when the well-meaning parent tries to solve the problem by personally approaching the accused bully or contacting their parents. They don't stop long enough to realise that an aggressive threat against another person constitutes bullying itself. Such a deed could even result in legal action. A response of this type more often than not complicates the problem and the school can be suddenly faced with a number of angry parents all demanding action on an issue that the school previously had little or no knowledge of.

Most parents are naturally defensive of their children and when contacted by the well-meaning parent of a 'professing victim', they could be excused for feeling the need to rise up and protect their child, or at least ensure that the facts are correct. If parents are going to take this approach they need to carefully choose their words if a positive, cooperative outcome is hoped for. It is far better to let the school deal with the issue according to policy and procedures. In such a case where parents become involved the victim no longer has to deal only with the bully, they now have to contend with the bully's parents and family as well. When a bullying child feels the support and backing of their parent, they are less likely to be cooperative with the school.

In responding to one such incident it took quite some time to convince the parents to agree to leave the issue with the school. There were threats and reminders from both families: 'If the school doesn't fix things quickly then we will take matters into our own hands.' Fortunately all the students involved understood the situation. A *shared responsibility* meeting took place and the desired result was achieved immediately. The normal follow-ups took place over three weeks and confirmed an end to the problem. However, such complications can impact on the effectiveness of any system, given the possible variation in personality types.

Bullying has never been solved by bullying. This type of intervention by parents can only make the situation more complicated and place the victim under further pressure.

Even when a student has been advised to retaliate, and in some cases has acted upon this advice, the *shared responsibility* meeting has proven to be effective. Listening to the parents and explaining to them the school policy and procedures goes a long way in supporting them and helps alleviate their worry and concern. The goal is to get all the people working together towards the same objectives. The objectives are to help the recipient to be safe, feel safe and to stop the bullying. It has been my experience that getting the parents to work with the school has been more challenging than getting the students to share in their responsibility. They usually say something like, 'Well, I will let you give it a try, but believe me, if you don't put an end to it, then I will.' Fortunately the students have been a dream to work with in comparison.

One angry parent said to me, after his daughter had been refusing to come to school for a week as a result of bullying, 'If this system can fix the problem then I will personally write to the Principal endorsing the method and strongly recommend that all schools take it up.' The girl was back at school in two days and the problem disappeared. I'm not sure if the letter ever arrived.

Well-meaning teachers can also cause complications when they bypass the approved school procedures and attempt to deal with bullying issues in their own way. Threats such as, 'If this doesn't stop, I'll ...,' are largely ineffective. Detentions and angry outbursts, very rarely produce the desired objectives. Private, unstructured, friendly 'off the record' chats with an accused bully, are often quickly forgotten or not taken seriously. Aggressive intervention often pushes the bullying further underground and diminishes any confidence that the recipient may have had in the school to help.

Unfortunately some of the old style teachers learnt to teach and survive using bullying tactics and have found it difficult to change. Teachers who tell students to 'toughen up', or 'stop telling tales', or 'don't be a wuss', need to catch up with the modern and legal world.

Such complications can be frustrating and make the *shared responsibility* meeting a little more challenging to manage. I advise that you just follow the procedure as outlined. Listen to any concerns the students may raise in relation to other staff, and stick to procedure. Be professional at all times. Do not criticise, put down, or engage in conversation about other staff members. If the issue needs to be followed through, take it up privately with the school administration who are responsible for all policies and procedures being followed correctly. It is important that there is a whole school approach if any anti-bullying program is to realise its full potential.

Some parents and teachers need to have their quest for justice or revenge satisfied. They find it difficult to accept that the person doing the wrong thing gets off free, that is, without punishment. I can understand this. This method acknowledges that people do learn from consequence and it allows the freedom for the school to impose consequences if and when it feels appropriate, even for a first offence. However, I do not advise this, as I believe premature consequences have the potential to reduce the effectiveness of the method. When a student is punished without being given an opportunity to learn and put things right, the entire psychology of the system is changed.

These concerns are often alleviated when it is explained that discipline and consequences form an important part of the overall policy and procedures. Should there be repeat offences there will be appropriate consequences and further action will be taken by the school.

It is impossible to list all the possible complications that you may face when dealing with bullying in schools. I have mentioned only a few, mainly to make the point 'stick to the system', no matter what, 'stick to the system'. In dealing with all cases of bullying the objectives remain the same.

They are:
- to help the recipient to be safe,
- to help the recipient feel safe,
- to stop the bullying.

Shared responsibility has proven to be extremely effective, even when faced with complications.

Conclusion

Thank you for reading this book and showing an interest in helping to solve the bullying problem in our schools. I'm sure if we work together and share the responsibility we will make a serious impact on it. If you would like further information or support for your school, I can be contacted at ifindley@yahoo.com.

Loneliness and the feeling of being unwanted is the most terrible poverty[6].

----

[6] Mother Teresa.

PART TWO

Appendices

APPENDIX ONE

CHECK LIST   Is this Bullying?

Are the bullying behaviours exhibited from one party or both?	One party	Both
Is the behaviour ongoing or is it a one-off?	Ongoing	One-off
Is the behaviour causing distress, fear, feelings of being unsafe, unhappiness or sadness?	Yes	No
Is there an imbalance of power? (strength, age, numbers, popularity)	Yes	No
Does the recipient have the ability and/or skills to defend themselves?	Yes = bullying	No = conflict or behavioural offence

SHARED RESPONSIBILITY MEETING FORM

Incident number: (circle)   1   2   3   4

Person holding interview: _____

Name of student: _____

Date: _____

Name of other students in group:

_____   _____

_____   _____

_____   _____

_____   _____

Name of student with concern: _____   Home Group: _____

Impact Statement:

_____

_____

_____

_____

_____

_____

_____

_____

Outline of Concern:

_____

_____

_____

_____

Concern identified through (circle)

Survey   Student   Parent   Teacher   Other

Date of Survey: _____

Indicate if the interviewed student was   Co-operative _____   Unco-operative _____

Action: Record what the student has decided to do to help solve the problem:

_____

_____

_____

_____

_____

Follow up   Date: _____   Student with concern   OK   Not OK

                                                  Interviewed student   OK   Not OK

Teacher comment or outcome:

_____

_____

_____

SHARED RESPONSIBILITY SAFETY SURVEY SHEET What is Bullying?

Name: _____   Home Group: _____

Date of Survey: _____

In your opinion are the behaviours listed below bullying? (Circle YES or NO)

Mark on the scale of 1–10 how you think a person might feel if they were the target of this behaviour.

1 is OK (no big deal) and 10 is very angry or upset.

Name calling	YES	NO	1	2	3	4	5	6	7	8	9	10
Pushing or punching	YES	NO	1	2	3	4	5	6	7	8	9	10
Making threats	YES	NO	1	2	3	4	5	6	7	8	9	10
Spreading rumours	YES	NO	1	2	3	4	5	6	7	8	9	10
Deliberately leaving others out	YES	NO	1	2	3	4	5	6	7	8	9	10
Making fun of others	YES	NO	1	2	3	4	5	6	7	8	9	10
Writing nasty notes	YES	NO	1	2	3	4	5	6	7	8	9	10
Pulling faces	YES	NO	1	2	3	4	5	6	7	8	9	10
Rude comments	YES	NO	1	2	3	4	5	6	7	8	9	10
Comments about a person's clothes	YES	NO	1	2	3	4	5	6	7	8	9	10
Comments about a person's looks	YES	NO	1	2	3	4	5	6	7	8	9	10
Mimicking (copying)	YES	NO	1	2	3	4	5	6	7	8	9	10
Tripping	YES	NO	1	2	3	4	5	6	7	8	9	10
Dirty looks	YES	NO	1	2	3	4	5	6	7	8	9	10
Blocking someone's path	YES	NO	1	2	3	4	5	6	7	8	9	10
Prank phone call or SMS messages	YES	NO	1	2	3	4	5	6	7	8	9	10
Taking money	YES	NO	1	2	3	4	5	6	7	8	9	10
Interfering with property	YES	NO	1	2	3	4	5	6	7	8	9	10

CONFIDENTIAL SAFETY SURVEY Preamble

You are about to be given a survey seeking your assistance in gaining information concerning your feelings of safety and comfort as a student at [*name of school*].

The information you give is anonymous and will not be traced back to you.

You are not to put your name on the survey and we advise that you do not tell anyone else what you have written.

This school endeavours to provide a comfortable and safe environment where you can contribute and learn, free from intimidation and harassment.

[Definition of Bullying]

Bullying is deliberate, ongoing behaviour that causes another person distress and it may be displayed in varying forms. Bullying is an abuse of power. It may be physical, verbal, or more indirect. People who engage in these sorts of activities need assistance in learning and developing skills that will enable them to contribute to our community in a more positive manner.

- There is to be no talking during this survey.
- There will be no communication with other students during this survey.
- Students are to sit in a position where no other student can see their survey.
- Students are advised not to talk about this survey afterwards with other students. This will help to keep everything confidential.
- No questions will be answered by the supervising teacher. If there is something you do not understand read the question again and if you still do not understand just do the best you can or leave it blank.

In completing this survey please be courageous, open and honest. This is your part in helping us make our school a better place for all. After you have completed the survey close it in half and hand it to the supervising teacher.

Thank you for your help.

CONFIDENTIAL SAFETY SURVEY

Gender: Male   Female

(Please circle your answer)

1	Do you feel safe at school?	YES NO
2	Have you felt unsafe at our school during the last 2 months?	YES NO
3	Have you been *treated badly* by other students at our school in the last 2 months?	YES NO
4	Are you being *treated badly* **now** by other students at our school?	YES NO
5	Have you seen other students being *treated badly* (by other students) in the last 2 months?	YES NO
6	Are there areas in our school where you feel uncomfortable in going?	YES NO

If YES, please mark these places on the school map below with an X

MAP

The chart below lists some bullying behaviours that have been known to cause discomfort and distress to students.

Please indicate if these things have been happening to you, or you have seen them happening to other students by placing ticks in the appropriate columns.

(You can tick both columns if necessary)

Behaviour	Happens to me	Seen it happen to others
Name calling		
Making threats		
Making fun of people		
Picking on the way a person looks		
Making fun of a person's clothes		
Putting a person down because they work hard or do well		
Mimicking (making fun of a person by smartly copying what they say or do)		
Spreading rumours		
Talking about a person behind their back (Back stabbing)		
Turning someone against someone else		
Getting yelled at by other students		
Making rude (sexual) comments		
Unwelcome and uninvited touching		
Rude drawings of body parts		
Giving dirty, greasy looks		
Pulling faces		
Writing nasty notes		
Taking or touching others' belongings without permission		
Using power to get favours or money		
Deliberately blocking someone's path		
Tripping		
Punching or kicking		
Bumping into people		

*Please help us help you by writing the names of any student in our school who is bullying you, or you have seen bullying others in the last 2 months. **Remember this is a private confidential survey and no information can be traced back to you.** We need your help to help us make and keep our school a safe place for everyone.*

_____   Year level or class _____

_____   Year level or class _____

_____   Year level or class _____

_____   Year level or class _____

_____   Year level or class _____

_____   Year level or class _____

APPENDIX TWO
RESEARCH

The *shared responsibility* method was developed and trialed for twelve months in an outer suburban Melbourne, co-educational, government, secondary college with a student population of 1030. This research enabled the school to measure the number of students reporting and engaging in bullying. It also indicated the year levels and gender of the perpetrators and the number of the students targeted, as well as the effectiveness of the program.

All the bullying incidents that were dealt with using the *shared responsibility* method in this twelve-month period resulted in positive outcomes. All incidents were followed up and monitored for a minimum of three weeks (usually longer).

The bullying incidents reported totalled 71 for the period.

Incident outcomes

Students who reported the bullying problem successfully solved:
- monitored over a three week period = 96%
- monitored over a six week period = 100%

When a victim of bullying indicated any uncertainty as to their feelings of safety the monitoring period was extended for a further three weeks. All students reported that the bullying had ceased but a few still expressed feelings of uneasiness and uncertainty after three weeks.

Students who bullied

Of the students who went through the process as bullies:
- 78% did not come up as engaging in bullying a second time.
- 22% engaged in further bullying but usually after a lengthy time gap and the offence was rarely against their original victim.
- only a few students bullied the same victim again. Follow up revealed that such problems usually involved an issue of dispute, conflict or other complication such as family quarrelling or a long-term unresolved dispute.
- only three students progressed to Stage 3 where parental assistance was sought.

These cases revealed personal and family issues that resulted in the appropriate support being offered and provided to the bullying student.

Success rate at Stage 1.	=	78%
Success rate at Stage 2.	=	20%
Students progressing to Stage 3.	=	2%
Students progressing to Stage 4.	=	0%

The research indicated that:

- boys bullying outnumbered girls 2 and a half to 1.
- bullying was most evident at Year 8, followed by Year 7, then Years 9, 10 and far less at Years 11 and 12.

The method proved effective dealing with students of both genders at all year levels. Research and data provided by the author.

School trials

I would like to acknowledge and thank the following people and their schools for their support and willingness to trial and provide feedback on the *shared responsibility* method of dealing with bullying. The method was trialed at both primary and secondary schools with positive results.

Schools that participated in the trials were:

Whittlesea Secondary College	November 2004 – November 2005 (12 months)
Whittlesea Primary School	October 2005 –November 2005 (5 weeks)
Broadmeadows Secondary College	October 2005 – November 2005 (5 weeks)

The names of the teachers involved:

Jenice Stokes	Leading Teacher Whittlesea Secondary College.
Mark Smit	Teacher Whittlesea Secondary College.
Melanie Hanlon	VCAL Coordinator Whittlesea Secondary College.
Sonia Reardon	Year 8 Coordinator Broadmeadows Secondary College.
Greg Handley	Pastoral Care Teacher Broadmeadows Secondary College.
Anna Radford	Junior School Coordinator & Student Welfare Coordinator Broadmeadows Secondary College.
John Coburn	Assistant Principal Whittlesea Primary School.
Pam Randall	Primary School Teacher Whittlesea Primary School.
Ian Findley	Chaplain Whittlesea Secondary College.

Since finalising this book many more teachers have been trained in the method and other schools have requested inservicing and staff training.

Commendations

The *shared responsibility* method of dealing with incidents of bullying has been trialed in both primary and secondary schools. The following comments have been provided by staff members who have been trained in the method and were willing to trial it in their school and provide feedback.

When trying to resolve a bullying incident, I have found myself accusing the bullies, disbelieving or blaming the victim and acting as an investigator, judge and jury. I have found that the *shared responsibility* method released me from this and enabled me to get the bullies and the victim onside in a non-threatening way. The students are treated with respect and dignity. Focusing on the victim, listening to the victim and giving them the opportunity to share the impact the bullying was having on them reassured them that they were being believed and taken seriously. When the impact of their behaviour on the victim was shared with the bullies, they were able to empathise with the victim and when their help was sought in helping to find a solution to the problem, the bullies were empowered to take steps to solve the problem. The solution came from them not me as the teacher. The consistent follow up resulted in the bullies and the victim being accountable for following through with their offers of help and actually experiencing success in finding a solution to the problem.

As a leading teacher I have seen students' lives, both those of the victims and the bullies, turned around in ways that I have not seen before in my 30 years of teaching. Students who were helpless victims of cruel, unrelenting bullying now are safe and bullies have stopped bullying.

I am excited about the *shared responsibility* method as it is 'beating bullying' in our school and has the potential to do so in all Australian schools.

Jenice Stokes. Leading Teacher. WSC.

I have always had a keen interest in understanding and preventing bullying. At university I studied extensively on the causes of bullying and characteristics of victims. This past year I have been trained and have worked with Ian Findley in applying the *shared responsibility* method in our school. I have found this approach to be extremely effective in dealing with the needs, concerns and welfare of the students involved. *Shared responsibility* has been an enormous success at WSC in reducing the rates of repeat offenders of bullying.

Mark Smit. Teacher. WSC.

I have been trained in *shared responsibility* and have had the opportunity to practise the method on several occasions. I have found this method to be incredibly effective, allowing both the victim and the perpetrator to feel a sense of empowerment. I believe the solution-focused approach to be the reason behind the amazing success of the sessions I have participated in.

The method has also allowed me to build constructive and positive relationships with students. I was extremely surprised and uplifted after one particular *shared responsibility* session, when I went into the school yard and one of the students who had been in the session as a 'bully' approached me to say hello and ask how I was. I now often talk at length with that student and have been extremely moved by her attitude.

It is my opinion that all schools should adopt the *shared responsibility* method and all teachers should have training in the method.

Melanie Hanlon. VCAL Coordinator. WSC.

I am the Year 8 Coordinator in a multicultural school in Melbourne's northern suburbs, which has approximately 650 students. This community has high rates of unemployment, broken families and many students from non-English speaking backgrounds. Despite the introduction of an anti-bullying action group and ongoing education programs in our school, bullying has been an ongoing problem for some time, particularly in the junior levels. Simply punishing the bullies was not working. In accepting the challenge to trial the *shared responsibility* method, I was hoping to gain an understanding of the process and discover a method that is truly effective in stopping bullying and dealing with bullying incidents. I found the method clear and easy to understand. The steps are easy to follow and the paper work/documentation I found very helpful. I had the opportunity to use this method with students at both Year 7 and Year 8 level. As outlined in the method, there are three main objectives. They are to ensure the victim is safe, feels safe, and to stop the bullying. I really like this method, particularly because it focuses on support for the victim and the impact the bullying is having on them. I found the method was extremely easy to follow, worked very well in our school and to be an effective method of dealing with incidents of bullying. The detailed documentation is an excellent record to have on file if further bullying was to continue. I believe that *shared responsibility* could easily be adopted by our school as the accepted practice in dealing with incidents of bullying.

Sonia Reardon. Year 8 Coordinator. BSC.

I am a 'Pastoral Care' teacher in a State Secondary College with high numbers of ESL (English as a Second Language) students and high EMA (Educational Maintenance Allowance) allocations. I have found it depressing when you think you have had a successful outcome with an incident of bullying, only to find the bully reoffends shortly afterwards. I like the way *shared responsibility* has a 'built in' way of dealing with repeat offenders. I found this method to be a well thought out, well constructed, easy way to 'approach/handle' all types of bullying. Our policy has always been to 'deal' with the bully—the victim tends to have been forgotten. *Shared responsibility* focuses on both. I have used this method with students ranging in age from 13–15 years and found that it worked very well. It has a very clear process with well established stages.

Greg Handley. Pastoral Care Teacher. BSC.

I like the positive approach, that it is a collective response and that the bully is empowered to change his/her behaviour voluntarily.

Anna Radford. Junior School/Student Welfare Coordinator. BSC.

In my capacity as Assistant Principal in a State Primary School I am required to deal with incidents of bullying as they arise. I found *shared responsibility* a common sense, no fuss approach which gets to the heart of the bullying problem. The non-accusing method is definitely a strong point. This gets all the parties on side and provides a basis to move forward and give a deeper understanding of the impact and ramifications of bullying. This method assists the students to take responsibility for their actions. This is a wonderful, inspiring approach that is adaptable and suitable for students of all ages, both Primary and Secondary.

John Coburn. Assistant Principal. WPS.

I teach in a semi-rural Primary School of approximately 430 students. I was keen to trial this new method of dealing with incidents of bullying and I worked with children between the ages of 6–8 years. I found it worked really well. Students were surprisingly open about their feelings and it revealed that some had private misgivings about how they had acted. I discovered that students are generally not aware of how others feel and the action–reaction connection. Students also feel empowered when they are able to discuss openly in a 'safe' forum. *Shared responsibility* seems to be a realistic approach to the bullying problem, which enables students to develop proactive life skills. I believe that this is an excellent form of 'open counselling' that could be used throughout the entire school.

Pam Randall. Primary School Teacher. WPS.

After having endured bullying while I was at school, I was totally dismayed to find that my daughter was suffering the same torment. Previous complaints while attended to, did not solve the problem and I was at my wits' end. My daughter came home in tears one day and I realised that going to the school was not an option until I had some sort of evidence that the bullying was ongoing. I gave my daughter a diary and asked that she note down things that had occurred and perhaps why the bullying may have been occurring. I planned to present this to the school and try and devise a plan to beat the thuggery.

There was one instance that was quite traumatic and my daughter was pulled from class and sent to you. At the time I doubted that your intervention would ease the problem but I stand corrected. You phoned me and explained that you may be able to help my daughter with this new *shared responsibility* method working with both the bullied and the bully. I agreed to try this as I was extremely concerned that if something was not done I would be forced to move schools.

You met with my daughter on several occasions and although she didn't discuss these meetings with me she was smiling again and the bullies had ceased tormenting her. The turnabout was completely and utterly amazing!

To say that I have my happy daughter back with me is an understatement. My daughter who I thought I had lost to the black hole of the 'secondary school and the teenage years' is happy and content.

To say thank you is almost not enough, I am in debt to you for allowing my daughter to continue her schooling at a school which I believe has truly addressed the issue of bullying that plagued me and countless others during my formative years.

Parent. WSC.